D1542332

Icons *of* Women's Style

Published in 2015 by
Laurence King Publishing Ltd
361–373 City Road
London EC1V 1LR
e-mail: enquiries@laurenceking.com
www.laurenceking.com

Text © 2014 Josh Sims
This book was designed and produced by
Laurence King Publishing Ltd, London.

Josh Sims has asserted his right under the Copyright, Designs and
Patents Act of 1988 to be identified as the author of this work.

All rights reserved. No part of this publication may be reproduced or
transmitted in any form or by any means, electronic or mechanical,
including photocopy, recording or any information storage and
retrieval system, without prior permission in writing from the publisher.

A catalogue record for this book is available

from the British Library.

ISBN: 978-1-78067-271-7

Design: Eleanor Ridsdale
Picture research: Tom Broadbent
Commissioning Editor: Helen Rochester
Senior Editor: Sophie Wise

Cover image: Grace Kelly, c. 1955. © By Howell Conant / Bob
Adelman Books.

Printed in China

Icons *of* Women's Style

Josh Sims

Laurence King Publishing

CONTENTS

INTRODUCTION 6

1.
OUTERWEAR 10
trench coat 12
riding jacket 16
leather jacket 18
cape 22

2.
SKIRTS 24
miniskirt 26
pencil skirt 30
circle skirt 34
skirt suit 36

3.
DRESSES 40
little black dress 42
empire-line dress 46
shift dress 48
halter-neck dress 52
prairie dress 56
wrap dress 58
shirt dress 62
kaftan 64
A-line dress 66
pleated dress 70

4.
TROUSERS 72
leather trousers 74
palazzo pants 78
leggings 80
culottes 82
jeans 84
hot pants 88
trouser suit 92
harem pants 96
Capri pants 98
pajama pants 100

5.
TOPS 102
Breton top 104
blouse 108
twinset 112
crop top 114
T-shirt 118
tube top 120

6.
UNDERWEAR 122
tights 124
bra 126
slip 130
corset 134

7.
LEISURE AND SWIMWEAR 136
swimming costume 138
bikini 142
jumpsuit 144
leotard 148

8.
SHOES 150
stiletto 152
platform 156
ballet pump 158
riding boot 162
sandal 166
plimsoll 170
cowboy boot 172
kitten heel 176
peep-toe & slingback 178
wedge 180

9.
ACCESSORIES 182
silk scarf 184
cloche 188
costume jewellery 190
it bag 194
beret 198

further reading 201
index 202
picture credits 206

Above: Mainbocher corset in Horst P. Horst's
iconic photograph for *Vogue*, 1939.
Opposite: A blue velvet dress suit worn with
pearls and yellow pumps in the 1940s.

INTRODUCTION

'Only the shallow don't judge by appearance'. Oscar Wilde's witticism is perhaps more true today than it has ever been – fashion is a global business enjoyed by more women than ever before. And, while trends come and go, there is more opportunity to dress with individuality, cherry-picking from a century or more of styles.

The choice is huge. While menswear tends to be based on a core canon of certain garments – changing in detail but remaining consistent in essence – womenswear is often founded on design innovation and the desire not so much for continuity as for the radically new.

Over the last 80 or so years in particular, thanks to the advent of truly global markets and communications, individual designers have been able to shape the wardrobes of millions of women in extreme ways (and certainly in ways of which menswear designers could only dream). The philosophy of the most pioneering womenswear designers has been less concerned with functionality than with, at its most basic, fun – the fun of dressing up, the fun of change for change's sake. It is, as Wilde hinted, superficial – in a good way. The best designs have both lasted and become the foundations on which new ideas in fashion can be built.

Certainly some designs have proven more enduring and more influential than others but each one shown in this book can lay claim to being an icon. Some are more likely to take us on a nostalgia trip than others – these fashions from the past, having lived through their introduction, may have been considered by many to be best left in the past. Yet, time and again, they have proven themselves to be fresh and exciting for new generations that have rediscovered them, either as a result of a designer delving into a company's archives or as a result of some personality of that generation making their own personal voyage into fashion history, perhaps via the vintage-clothing market.

These designs have often had an impact far greater than might have been expected, at least when they were first shown – their seasonal moment in the sun. Since the story of women's fashion over the twentieth century is also that of the changing role of women in society, these icons have sometimes also reflected, and sometimes even shaped, changes in the way we think: about women in the workplace or about women's sexuality, for example.

From women in trousers to those in power suits, miniskirts or barely-there bikinis, to those toting certain bags – often more totems of status than something to carry stuff in – or certain attitudes, from the romantic to the radical, the androgynous to the sometimes strange, a single style of clothing has been seen over and over to do much more than merely provide a covering. Fun, it seems, can have meaning too.

Opposite: Twiggy and another model in 1960s mini dresses.
Above: Audrey Hepburn in a little black dress, c. 1955.

1.

OUTERWEAR

trench coat / riding jacket / leather jacket / cape

TRENCH COAT

When George Peppard's distressed would-be lover finally embraces Audrey Hepburn's Holly Golightly in the 1961 film *Breakfast at Tiffany's* (Blake Edwards), it is in the pouring rain. A good job, then, that she is wearing a trench coat. The sartorial star of the film is, of course, Golightly's little black dress (see p.42), which made Hepburn a style icon. However, the image of her in what until then had been perceived as a predominantly male garment also created a stir, despite, or perhaps because of, her petite figure, certainly the cinched-in waist helped to find favour among women. Sales of the coat to women rocketed, establishing it as a fashion classic, soon after given added cudos when Jacqueline Kennedy Onassis, Joanne Woodward and Brigitte Bardot (in *Une Ravissante Idiote*, Edward Molinaro, 1964) were all spotted wearing the trench.

This was, however, the second wave of popularity for the trench coat. Women had worn them before, notably during the early 1920s, as much as a statement of emancipation as of fashion. Again, it was stars of the screen portraying the strong woman archetype who wore the trench: Greto Garbo on the set of *A Woman of Affairs* (Clarence Brown, 1928), Gloria Swanson in *Queen Kelly* (Erich von Stroheim, 1929) and Bette Davis in of *Human Bondage* (John Cromwell, 1934). The trench coat continued to be used to signal a sassy mannishness – Katharine Hepburn wore an outsized trench coat in *The Iron Petticoat* (Ralph Thomas, 1956), for example – right up until Audrey Hepburn's feminization of the garment.

Burberry, a co-inventor of the style, made the coat in *Breakfast at Tiffany's*. The post-World War II period might have seen Hollywood leading men and sometimes ladies – the likes of Robert Mitchum, Ava Gardner and Humphrey Bogart – trying to pass off the trench coat as somehow quintessentially American (not to mention, the default choice

Opposite: A model keeping dry in a Weatherbee trench coat in the middle of a field in Switzerland.
Below left: Catherine Deneuve and Nino Castelnuovo in *The Umbrellas of Cherbourg* (1964).
Below right: Audrey Hepburn and George Peppard in *Breakfast at Tiffany's* (1961).

A dramatically lit *Vogue* studio portrait of the
French film actress Annabella.

of the hardbitten film-noir detective type), but it is a British invention, belonging jointly, despite their rivalry over it, to Aquascutum and Burberry. The former invented the first waterproof wool, devised a field coat for soldiers of the Crimean War (1853–56) and would later corner the market for trench coats in the movies. Meanwhile, draper Thomas Burberry invented gabardine in 1879 and won the contract to supply a trench-type raincoat for the Boer Wars and beyond.

One of the oldest army garments still widely worn, the trench coat was devised as a means of keeping the endless mud off uniforms in the trenches of World War I, although it was allowed to be worn only by officers. This explains the epaulettes, which remain today, there to attach the insignia of one's rank. The raglan sleeves came with wrist straps, the D-ring at the waist was used to hook on ammunition packs and other equipment and the storm flap at the shoulder, while letting the rain run away from the body, also helped soften rifle recoil.

Such concerns were undoubtedly not a priority for actresses Charlotte Rampling, Catherine Deneuve or Charlotte Gainsbourg, each of whom made the trench coat part of their style, as well as ensuring the garment remains central to the idea of French chic. In later decades, Kate Moss modelled the style in advertising campaigns for Burberry, while Victoria Beckham and Kate Middleton (the Duchess of Cambridge) also became fans. Few items have stood the test of time in the woman's wardrobe like the trench coat. It has proved a staple that can be reinvented time and again, whether by introducing bright colours or contrast sleeves or adding to, or reducing, the original ten front buttons.

Below left: Kate Middleton, Duchess of Cambridge, on a windswept royal visit in 2011. **Right:** American dancer, actress and long-term professional partner to Fred Astaire, Ginger Rogers, c. 1943.

RIDING JACKET

Top: An 1884 *Vanity Fair* illustration of Elisabeth of Bavaria, wife of Emperor Franz Joseph of Austria, wearing a riding habit.
Bottom: Alice and Nancy Whitney, daughters of American financier Richard Whitney, dressed to ride at the Far Hills Horse Show in New Jersey, 1933.

When Vivienne Westwood launched her 'Harris Tweed' collection in Autumn/Winter 1987, it was less her reinvigoration of what had come to be regarded as a fusty fabric that was most interesting, and more her suggestion of Englishness, or, at least, the stereotype evoked by the aristocratic enclaves of country houses and boarding schools, of hunting, shooting and fishing.

And, hunting in particular. While other designers such as Ralph Lauren used riding jackets to portray an upper-class Englishness, Westwood reworked red barathea and Tattersall check versions to hint at what was the supposedly very English repressed sexuality under all that trim, formal tailoring. Hers was the suggestion of the riding-crop-wielding dominatrix, similarly worked by Jilly Cooper in her novels *Riders* (1985) and *Polo* (1991). Small wonder, then, that this interplay between the prim and the passionate has made the riding jacket a womenswear staple.

The story of the riding jacket was initially more one of imitating male riding attire. As early as the seventeenth century, a well-to-do woman – which one would have to be to own a horse, to ride and to pay a tailor to make clothes especially to ride in – might wear a doublet, or, later, what was known as a justacorps (a full-skirted, knee-length coat introduced to men's fashion by Charles II in 1666), typically in silk brocade and complete with plenty of expensive decoration, from heavy embroidery to gold braiding.

It was not until the 1730s that the jacket began to resemble the tailored garment of today and, while still based on the male version, also began to be adapted for female fashion. The jacket was generally worn undone, fastened only over the chest by a hook and eye, and had small cuffs and button-back revers, just like a fashionable man's riding jacket of the time. It was even worn in the colours of the wearer's husband's regiment, but it did have a much wider skirt to make room for the hooped dresses worn underneath. This flared peplum grew and shrunk over the decades as women's skirts became more or less full.

By the end of the eighteenth century, riding jackets were following women's fashion more closely: when the high-waisted empire line came in, jackets were dramatically shortened to end just under the bust. The masculine elements remained, however, for example, true to military uniform, buttons in single or double rows down the front of the jacket made for a typical design. If, instead, a woman chose to ride wearing a redingote – a full-length coat dress – it would have been made by a man's tailor and consequently retained a more mannish look.

Come the early twentieth century, riding jackets were again more or less interpretations of those worn by men: male riding fashion embraced a plain, short, boxy jacket known as a 'sack', and the woman's version followed suit, with a trimmed-down garment made more flattering by the addition of darts. Indeed, so flattering was the style that women began to wear it beyond the needs of equestrianism, and fashion colours, as opposed to the red, green or navy traditionally worn for riding, came in. The final signature characteristic of the woman's style came in around the 1930s, when the front of the jacket was cut away to prevent it from rubbing against the saddle.

A model in tartan riding jacket and kilt by Vivienne Westwood, a designer who has made riding clothes something of a signature.

LEATHER JACKET

The leather jacket is the most masculine of garments. Notwithstanding the leather itself – typically tough, shiny and shell-like – the connotations are those of historically male enclaves, from biker gangs to the military. So perhaps it would require a subculture as combative as punk to bring the leather jacket into the woman's wardrobe. For punk, the garment's hints of the fetishistic – notably biker jackets with their zips, belts and stiff leather – only added to its rebellion against societal norms, be that commercialism, conservatism or gender-specific dress. The heavily customized black leather jacket was as much an anti-establishment symbol for Jordan, the famously haughty manager of punk pioneers Vivienne Westwood and Malcolm McLaren's London shop Sex, or for Siouxsie Sioux, as it was for the Sex Pistol's Sid Vicious. Another subculture – grunge – would underscore the biker jacket's unisexuality in the 1990s: the poster for *Singles* (Cameron Crowe, 1992), one of the period movies about grungy twenty-somethings, featured Bridget Fonda and Matt Dillon, both in biker jackets.

This was all despite the fact that the classic biker jacket, the Perfecto, was made famous by one of the most male characters in movie history: Marlon Brando's Johnny in *The Wild One* (Laslo Benedek, 1953), nihilistic leader of a biker gang. The Perfecto, designed and made by Irving Schott of Schott Bros, initially for a Long Island Harley Davidson dealership, was the first jacket to be fastened by a zip. With its epaulettes, studs, collar snaps and horsehide, not to mention its popularity among hardcore bikers, from rockers to greasers, it screamed macho, if not trouble.

A similar story might be told of the other key pieces of leather jacket design, the templates for so many copies, from the sheepskin-collared, dark brown Irvin jacket issued to bomber crews of the RAF during World War II to the russet A2 pilot's jacket created for the US Army

Opposite: Rocker and singer Chrissie Hynde, front woman for The Pretenders, in leather gear in 1979.
Below left: The poster for the film *Singles* (1992) – helping to make the leather jacket a staple of grunge.
Below right: An all-leather style from French designer Claude Montana for his A/W 1996/97 collection.

Air Corp. The latter was designed in 1930 and remained standard issue to American military pilots until 1943, but then, flouting regulations, was retained by many who had become so attached to the jackets that they were still being worn on active service during the Korean War, which ended a decade later in 1955.

If punk co-opted the biker style for wear by women, then it was the more military influence of designer fashion during the 1980s that kept it in vogue. Cropped versions appeared, as did those with shoulder pads, or a slimmed-down look. Leather was softer, more luxurious and sometimes much more colourful for women to wear. Yves Saint Laurent had been two decades ahead of his time by showing a black leather jacket as part of his 'Beat' collection in the 1960s. But, it would take designers Giorgio Armani, Gianni Versace, Azzedine Alaïa, Thierry Mugler and Chanel to successfully tweak the leather jacket to give it more feminine appeal, without entirely losing the suggestion of outsider edginess.

Left: The customized leather biker jacket became a punk staple – as worn here in Chelsea, London, in 1984.
Below: Popstar Rihanna performs in a cropped leather jacket at the MTV Awards in 2008.
Opposite: French singer Françoise Hardy wearing a fashion take on the biker jacket for actual motorbiking, in 1969.

CAPE

In its most basic form, requiring little more than a section of woollen fabric thrown over the shoulders, the cape or cloak and variations on it – the mantle or dolman, for example, or, in lighter form, a stole from the 1960s or a pashmina from the 1990s – have featured in the way we dress for millennia. The Romans wore them ('cloak' comes from the Latin *cloca*), although it was not until the Renaissance that they became a more fitted garment, tailored around the shoulders, akin to an opera cloak. The cape offered immediate practicality – a warm, encompassing cover – which was the main reason any woman would have worn a floor-length hooded cloak during the sixteenth and seventeenth centuries, and why the cloak featured as part of the uniform of service women and nurses until well into the twentieth century. But it has also suggested mystery, the stuff of spies, superheroes, wizards and witches, and romance, of princes and princesses.

Variations in length, textile and trimming gave capes a certain kind of stylishness in their time; Victorian women might have worn a cloak because it covered their wide skirts or to disguise pregnancy, but come the big freeze that hit England in 1861, for example, a sealskin or velvet pile cloak became the look for women of means. But, such was its firm place in the history of so many societies, it was not until 1911 that it underwent its first true consideration as a fashion item, just when it was going out of everyday wear thanks to the introduction of oriental-style cocoon coats that provided the same top-to-toe protection. This was when Parisian couturier Paul Poiret created a velvet, fur-collared and cuffed batik cape with a swirl pattern. He returned to the style in 1919, when he created the 'Tanger', an ethnic-inspired cape.

That, of course, looked to another cloak-like form of covering – the poncho. Traditionally a rectangular piece of heavy material with a hole through which the head passed, rather than going around the shoulders, it was sometimes defined as the 'South American cloak'. Ponchos were originally handwoven in bold, broad-weave stripes by the continent's ancient civilizations, the Incas and Aztecs, and it was through the Spanish conquistadores that the style made its way to Europe, although fashionable Spaniards of the time preferred to wear theirs in plain fabrics. Come the mid-1960s, while Clint Eastwood in Sergio Leone's spaghetti westerns did much to revive interest in it, just as important was the hippy movement that embraced the poncho for its authenticity, as an expression of admiration for native peoples or as a souvenir of exotic travels. As Frank Zappa would ask in the song 'Camarillo Brillo', 'Is that a real poncho, I mean is that a Mexican poncho or is that a Sears poncho?'

Fashion designers inevitably picked up on the look for its graphic appeal and suggestion of bohemianism; through the 1960s and 1970s, Pucci, Bill Gibb and Missoni produced various versions, with fringing, crochet, leather trimming and beading, as part of a pot-pourri of references that encompassed Andean, Indian and Native American arts. Diehards wore only an original, a 'rancid poncho' perhaps, as Zappa sang in the same song. Fashion soon moved on, but revisited the poncho in the early twenty-first century, when Dolce & Gabbana, Mark Montano, Alexander McQueen and Hermès again tapped the boho aesthetic.

Top: Capes from the Christian Dior A/W collection of 1971/72, modelled in London. **Bottom:** On the streets in Sweden in 1971, home-made knitted capes proving to be a hippy style for colder climates

A fashion model of 1954, her cropped cape
part of an all-red ensemble.

2.

SKIRTS

miniskirt / pencil skirt / circle skirt / skirt suit

MINISKIRT

Quite who came up with the idea of the miniskirt remains open to debate. Was it British designer Mary Quant, whose design of 1965 was inspired by her childhood love of ballet attire and named after Alex Issigonis's groundbreaking Mini car? She daringly took hemlines well above the knee, tapping into the street style of 'Swinging London' and the women who visited her influential Kings Road shop Bazaar. Was it French designer André Courrèges, whose futuristic, space-age short skirt was shown to haute-couture customers in 1964? Was it John Bates, British founder of the Jean Varon label, costumier for the likes of Diana Rigg in the 1960s television series *The Avengers* and designer of even shorter skirts before either Courrèges or Quant? Or perhaps it was the ancient Egyptians, whose female performers wore something mid-thigh and very similar?

Regardless, the miniskirt was a sartorial summation of the 1960s: the growing gap – in attitude and in dress – between youth and the parental generation; an increased (sexual) liberation for women; and a readiness to challenge ossified rules of propriety. Witness the storm created when British model Jean Shrimpton attended the Melbourne Cup Carnival in Australia in 1965 without hat or gloves and, more radically, bare-legged in a white Colin Rolfe minidress. Or, when Brigitte Bardot arrived in London by jet wearing a plaid miniskirt in the same year, also bare-legged. It has been argued that the miniskirt was only socially feasible because of the advent of tights, and Quant's coloured and patterned tights, in particular, which made the wearing of stockings and garter belts unnecessary. Imagine the fuss when, in 1966, as part of his 'Body Jewellery' collection, Paco Rabanne introduced new versions of the miniskirt, including a semi-transparent one in plastic chain mail, another made from wire-linked metal discs and even a 'throw-away' minidress.

Opposite: Women from the British Society for the Protection of Mini Skirts protesting outside the House of Dior in London in September 1966, against its alleged 'unfair' treatment of miniskirts.
Below left: Mary Quant, one of the pioneers of the miniskirt, dressed in one in 1967.
Below right: The British model Twiggy wearing a tasselled minidress in a Native American style, ideal to wear on a TWA flight out of Heathrow Airport in the mid-1960s.

Like the hot pants that followed, the miniskirt suited fashion's feminine ideal of the time – tall, slender, boyish, leggy, even gawky – and Christian Dior and Yves Saint Laurent would also later lend their credibility to the design. For all that, it was certainly too much, or rather too little, for some. The miniskirt worn in the more puritanical USA was always longer than its European equivalent. 'Swinging London' was outrageous to visiting tourists, so much so that a 1967 television documentary from the American ABC network was called *The Miniskirt Rebellion*. In some countries, the skirt even prompted reported instances of violence against supposedly inappropriately dressed women.

Quant was disconcerted by these reactions: 'We thought we were designing clothes for our friends around Chelsea. It wasn't anticipated that it would have any effect. I didn't set out to shock [with the miniskirt]. I wanted to move and run, go to work then go on in the evening somewhere I could dance.'

For many, the miniskirt reflected an upbeat sense of new possibilities during the mid-1960s; it was a barometer of changing public mood. Indeed, it was a test of the theory that hemlines rise in economic boom times, disproven perhaps by the miniskirt's later, ironic adoption by punk during the 1970s, when it appeared in leather and PVC, with slashed tights or fishnet stockings. Yet, by the 1980s it again substantiated this theory by its inclusion in corporate female power dressing. As with any hemline, fashion was destined to periodically make the length unfashionable: by the end of the 1960s, for example, the mini was being upstaged by the calf-length midi-skirt. This was, in part, because the mini, now the micro-mini or pelmet, could not get any shorter without, as the joke had it, becoming a belt.

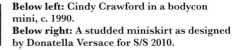

Below left: Cindy Crawford in a bodycon mini, c. 1990.
Below right: A studded miniskirt as designed by Donatella Versace for S/S 2010.

A metal minidress from the inventive French designer André Courrèges, modelled in 1965.

PENCIL SKIRT

Few garments in the woman's wardrobe scream the 1940s and 1950s as much as the pencil skirt. Cut straight from hip to hem just below the knee, creating a tube- or pencil-like garment, the skirt – designed by Christian Dior in the 1940s – may have been introduced as a consequence of rationing. If, for modesty's sake, the full skirts of the period could not be made shorter, then they could be made narrower, using less fabric in the process. Worn high on the waist and hugging the body (all the more so thanks to the consequent popularity of the corset), the pencil skirt became a definition of femininity. It emphasized the hourglass figure that was not only a welcome counter to the mannish factory clothes of wartime, but which also came to define glamour for the next two decades.

Dior's H-line skirt, as he called it (in contrast to the fuller A-line style of his post-war New Look), and similar skirts by Pierre Balmain and Jacques Fath were seen on women from office workers and secretarial staff to Hollywood stars Lauren Bacall, Grace Kelly and Elizabeth Taylor. The pencil skirt's sharp tailoring, especially when worn with a short jacket, fitted blouse or sweater, may have been superficially reserved, even prim, but deep down was strongly sexual. As Jack Lemmon's character Daphne was to approvingly sum up, the sassy, short-stepped movement of Marilyn Monroe in a pencil skirt in Billy Wilder's 1959 movie *Some Like It Hot*, was 'like Jell-O on springs'.

Fashion had, however, been here before: in the early years of the twentieth century, the hobble skirt, its name inspired by the restriction it imposed on taking long strides when walking, had become high style thanks to the birth of flight. When, in 1908, Wilbur and Orville Wright made their first flight with a passenger, they so impressed the wife of one of their associates, a Mrs Berg, that she asked for a ride. To protect her modesty, her long dress was tied to her legs above the ankles. The

Opposite: A model shows off a Dior creation from the 1950s.
Below left: Hollywood legend Marilyn Monroe strikes a 'Jell-O on springs' pose in 1952.
Below right: A Cecil Beaton fashion illustration featuring models, left to right, wearing outfits by Eva Lutyens, Sportscraft and Margaret Barry.

Pierre Balmain's S/S 1958 collection featured
what he called his 'tubular line' – a long, fitted
bodice with hip-hugging pencil skirt.

result was an image disseminated globally by the press that proved to be an inspiration to designers, most notably Paul Poiret who created a similar dress in 1910, closely fitted at the ankles. 'I have freed the bust from prison but I have put chains on the legs,' Poiret famously said.

It was a change in hemline length that brought the pencil skirt's most triumphant years to an end. The advent of Mary Quant's miniskirt in 1965 (see p.27) suddenly made the traditional pencil skirt look stiff and all too respectable. Indeed, it would not be until the 1980s that the pencil skirt would make a return, in part because of the retro-futurism of Ridley Scott's sci-fi movie *Bladerunner* (1982), but primarily as a component of a business suit. A corporate, 'power-shouldered', tightly waisted suit echoed the explosion in banking and financial services in that decade, for which the pencil skirt's respectability was just right. Of course, the style could still be suggestive when required, especially in black leather.

Dutch model Marpessa (on the left) photographed in Sicily in 1987 for a Dolce & Gabbana advertising campaign.

CIRCLE SKIRT

Top: In 1957 dressmaker Michael Nadler of Regent Street presented this traditional circle skirt, complete with a border pattern of frisky Cairn Terriers. The real Cairn Terrier was owned by the model.
Bottom: The circle skirt was beloved by American teenagers of the 1950s in part for its dynamism during dancing, especially jiving. Onlookers got a welcome eyeful of leg too.

Novelty might not be the best starting place for a wardrobe classic, but it worked for the circle skirt. In 1947, American actress, soprano singer and designer Juli Lynne Charlot decided to make a skirt inspired by the nipped-in waists and full-volume skirts of Christian Dior's New Look, the lifting of wartime rationing on fabric and the fact that her husband had just lost his job. Her idea was to make a skirt that comprised a plainly draped single circle of fabric, contrary to the trends for lightly gathered dirndl-like and fully pleated skirts. As such it was easy to make, with just one seam to arrange and no darts, pleats or gathers. This was essential to Charlot since, although she had designed all of her stage costumes, including those in which she performed as the straight woman to the Marx brothers, she could not sew.

Charlot decided to add interest to her design in the form of appliquéd shapes in felt, of which she had a limitless supply as her mother owned a factory that used felt. Such was the fun in the style, all the more so perhaps with World War II still a fresh memory, that a local Beverly Hills store bought and quickly sold all she had. It also suggested what she might put on her next batch: dog shapes. Charlot agreed, producing a run featuring three dachshunds performing a small story of canine flirtation and entwined leads – the designer liking the idea that her skirts would be conversation starters.

The next run featured poodles. It was this design that captured the public imagination and the 'poodle skirt' entered the fashion vernacular. The influential Bullocks Wilshire department store placed orders and even offered Charlot the store windows to show off her designs. Neiman Marcus and Bergdorf Goodman soon followed suit and bought her circle skirts in large enough quantities to allow her to set up her own factory.

The style was soon copied, less by other designers and more by women who easily made their own inexpensive versions, which meant, appealingly, that no two skirts were the same. This did not, however, prevent most of the major sewing-pattern companies publishing patterns for circle skirts, nor circle-skirt kits entering the market. Available from dime stores, these kits were cardboard tubes filled with the skirt fabric, printed with outlines for the felt pieces, which were also provided, along with the needle and thread with which to attach them. As such, by the early years of the 1950s the circle skirt was ubiquitous in the USA, especially among teenage girls; the skirt style, heavily advertised in such magazines as *Seventeen*, proved the ideal, swirling garment in which to move to the new jitterbug dance craze.

Other popular designs that appeared on the skirt were playing cards, vinyl records, cats, flowers, desert scenes (Charlot was particularly inspired by the Mexican landscape) and motifs from circus and cowboy lore, though some also added more sophisticated embroidery, sequins and beading, too. Adult women were more inclined to wear plain styles – the circle skirt may have been one of the first fashions with an age limit.

The circle skirt helped to define the 1950s in the USA, fitting in with its image as a decade of new, pastel-coloured domestic appliances, kitsch design, the positivity of a consumer boom and the birth of the housewife. This has ensured that whenever fashion revisits the 1950s, it invariably revisits the circle skirt, although the poodles are usually kept on a leash.

American film actress Jean Parker in a flowery
circle skirt, complete with petticoats, in 1953.

A model wearing a brown and white checked
rayon suit – tidy and professional but still
feminine in 1942.

SKIRT SUIT

Women have worn skirts with tailored jackets since the late nineteenth century when they began to live more active lifestyles and it became more widespread to wear what were then perceived as practical, streamlined garments. But, it was not until the 1930s and 1940s that the skirt suit – jacket and skirt matching with a rule-bound formality that had previously been the preserve of menswear – found popularity.

Two forces were at play, each powering the skirt suit into fashion or practical use throughout the decades. One was Hollywood, which saw a degree of experimentation in the cutting of women's skirt suits, resulting in striking designs such as that worn by Joan Crawford in *No More Ladies* (Edward H. Griffith, 1935), designed by Adrian Adolf Greenberg, complete with mid-calf skirt and a fitted jacket with outlandishly outsize lapels. Or, the dramatically cut, almost futuristic jackets with sculptural 'V-line' skirts, also by Greenberg, who was better known for show-stopping evening gowns.

Huge puff sleeves, butterfly collars, square shoulders with very fitted sleeves, asymmetric fastenings and distorted proportions were all at play. Ironically, such tailored outfits were considered ideal for travel – the 1930s saw the first boom in international tourism – albeit travel of a luxurious kind in which dressing up was still considered de rigeur. Christian Dior's influential pencil-skirt design of 1940 (see p.31) was introduced as part of a woman's suit ensemble.

If Hollywood lent the skirt suit a kind of glamour, and, since it could not follow fashion due to the risk of looking dated by the time a movie was released, also a sense of boldness, the other driving force was the much more mundane change in working patterns during the 1940s. Wartime led to more women entering the office space, initially as secretarial staff, and wartime rationing meant that most skirt suits were

Below left: A double-breasted skirt suit with a distinctive tie at the waist, designed by Balmain in 1954.
Below right: Designed by Jeanne Barrie, this 1944 rayon crepe suit, with jet buttons and peplum, is striking for its lime green shade.

simple and practical, with skirts cut just around the knee, although a striking V-shaped silhouette remained typical until the 1950s.

The 1950s saw a considerable softening of the suit as it made a return as a fashion garment rather than a workaday one. Gabrielle 'Coco' Chanel introduced one of her most famed garments, the woollen cardigan suit, a knee-length skirt with a version of the semi-structured cardigan jacket she had created in 1925, which found favour with the likes of Audrey Hepburn and Grace Kelly. Continually updated, the Chanel suit – often in tweed or wool jersey – with a slim skirt and collarless boxy jacket, trimmed in braid, with patch pockets and gold buttons, and with an internal chain that helped it hang properly from the shoulders, became one of the designer's biggest hits, helping her business make a return when it was relaunched in 1953 (having closed at the outbreak of World War II).

Throughout the 1960s it, and its many imitations, proved the archetype of the skirt suit, which was still being worn by an older generation of women or on more formal occasions by those whose role dictated it, for example, Jacqueline Kennedy. But such ladylike dressing – of a kind that had been exemplified by Hitchcock's leading ladies, Grace Kelly in *Rear Window* (1954) and Kim Novak in *Vertigo* (1958), for instance – was increasingly coming into conflict with a much looser, hippie-inspired style.

The skirt suit would not make a comeback until the 1980s and 1990s, again thanks to working women taking up executive positions within companies. Dubbed 'power suits', with their shoulder pads reminiscent of 1940s style, these semi-conformist creations had the benefit of drawing attention to the wearer's seriousness without expecting her to ape male dress. Books such as John Molloy's *Dress for Success* (1975) and *The Woman's Dress for Success Book* (1977), with its navy-suited, briefcase-carrying woman on the cover, championed the concept of dressing your way up the corporate ladder, as became part of the plot of the 1988 movie *Working Girl* (Mike Nichols).

A 1935 fashion illustration featuring the designs of Elsa Schiaparelli, one in a blue skirt suit with 'wildcat' fur gloves, the other with gross-point embroidered vest and seal fur skirt.

Prince William and Kate Middleton – in red wool skirt suit – on a royal visit to the University of St Andrews, Scotland, in 2011.

Blue, white and red Chanel skirt suits modelled in Paris, 1983.

3.

DRESSES

little black dress / empire-line dress / shift dress /
halter-neck dress / prairie dress / wrap dress / shirt dress /
kaftan / A-line dress / pleated dress

LITTLE BLACK DRESS

It may not sound like much of a compliment, but when American *Vogue* compared a dress illustrated on its pages to the Ford Model T car, it undoubtedly was. Both were revolutionary in their back-to-basics simplicity, and both were, as *Vogue* termed them, 'attainable': the dress stripped back ornamentation and reinstated black as the colour not of mourning but of sophisticated, elegant fashion (since dye was so expensive, black had actually been worn by Spanish aristocracy as early as the sixteenth century), while the car democratized personal transport.

The comparison was made in 1926, some 18 years after the launch of the car but nonetheless apt: it was the year that Gabrielle 'Coco' Chanel debuted her version of the dress that, arguably, proved to be her greatest contribution to fashion. Although the simple black dress had been experimented with before Chanel – by British couturier Edward Molyneux, for example – Chanel's was a striking, minimalistic, figure-hugging, knee-length jersey version with high neckline and long sleeves. It was Chanel herself who dubbed it her 'little black dress' (although 'little black frock' was a phrase used before in Henry James's *The Wings of the Dove* in 1902), with a familiarity and fondness that helped define it as the default style for almost any occasion, dressed up or down as required.

The design was ahead of its time, although it played a fitting part in the radical changes that womenswear underwent during the flapper era of the 1920s and beyond. Starlets, performers and royalty from Joan Bennett to Josephine Baker and Wallis Simpson, the Duchess of Windsor, wore some variation on the LBD, as the style came to be abbreviated, from those with peacock feathers to those with asymmetric necklines and diamanté embellishment. Over the following decades, black became an everyday part of women's wardrobes both

Opposite: The poster for *Breakfast at Tiffany's* (1961), the film that launched a thousand little black dresses.
Right: French actress Catherine Deneuve modeling an Yves Saint Laurent 'Rive Gauche' dress, 1966.

for reasons of practicality, especially the rationing in many countries during World War II, and for its growing reputation as the colour of sexiness – see Rita Hayworth in *Gilda* (Charles Vidor, 1946).

But the LBD was not to have its greatest, most defining moment until 1961, when Audrey Hepburn wore the style as Holly Golightly in *Breakfast at Tiffany's* (Blake Edwards). Only then did the little black dress undergo a transformation from wardrobe novelty to universal staple. And this despite the fact that the little black dress worn by Golightly in the opening credits, designed by long-time Hepburn collaborator Hubert de Givenchy, was not that little, being floor-length and worn with evening gloves. Elsewhere, Catherine Deneuve's dress in *Belle de Jour* (Luis Buñuel, 1967) would seal the dress's reputation for French chic. Synthetic fibres made the style available and affordable, and sheer fabrics such as tulle and netting began to be incorporated into the design.

In time, the LBD came to be a term applied to almost any black dress, the graphic directness and blank canvas of the shade, whether in silk, spandex or leather, proving more important than any particular cut. This was something that Jacqueline Kennedy Onassis recognized, seeing the dress as a means of expressing her love of accessories, notably her signature pillbox hat and outsize sunglasses. There would, however, be exceptions, most famously the Gianni Versace dress – very low cut, split down the side of the torso and fastened by giant gold safety pins – that actress Elizabeth Hurley wore to attend a movie premiere in 1994.

Below: Actor High Grant with Elizabeth Hurley wearing a Versace dress to a film premier in 1994 – newspaper headlines followed.
Right: A model wearing a black dress made from a *Vogue* pattern copied from a Paris original.

British actress Vivien Leigh in a studio portrait taken in 1940.

EMPIRE-LINE DRESS

In the twentieth century, the empire line has most commonly been associated with saucy lingerie thanks to a 1956 movie called *Baby Doll* (Elia Kazan), in which the main character appears in a short, busty nightgown. A decade later, the style would return in the form of a dress, no less short as the miniskirts and minidresses of the time dictated, but drawing no less attention to the décolletage either. In more streamlined, schoolgirlish versions, it had a certain modish appeal too – the supermodel of the period, Twiggy, wore the style – but its sexual undertones were not forgotten come the 1990s, when Hole's Courtney Love led something of a grunge revival of it. These undertones, however, cannot be further from the line's origins.

A fashionable interest in history can spark a style. The Georgian period of the 1790s through to the 1820s saw women not only wear less and less clothing – compared with the modesty-saving layers that went before – but also enjoy a fascination, in the arts and architecture as well as in fashion, for all things Roman and Grecian.

Drawing on both these things, fashion took the popular chemise shift and combined it with what it perceived as being the style of the ancient civilizations to create a full, free-flowing form of dress, akin to a nightgown, with short puff sleeves, a low neckline and a high waist. The skirt eventually draped from just below the bust, no longer making it necessary to emphasize the waspish waist through tight corsetry. The dresses '*à la grecque*', as the French called them, were often worn in white or pale pastel muslin or batiste, both of which required frequent and expensive laundering, making the dress an expression of wealth and status.

In keeping with the territorial ambitions of another icon of the times, the cut came to be referred to as the empire waist, or empire line, inspired by the empire building of France's Napoleon Bonaparte. He was a man well known for his efforts to promote the French fashion industry – almost destroyed during the French Revolution – not least through his wife Josephine, an ardent fan of French couturier Leroy. Bonaparte had fireplaces blocked and insisted no dress could be worn twice at court, all in a bid to make women buy more clothes: to protect their modesty a chemisette (a kind of half blouse) was worn during the day to cover the low neckline of empire-line dresses; a pelisse (a knee- or full-length, open-fronted lightweight coat, also empire line) might be worn over the dress, too.

Following notions of Greek classicism, empire-line dresses kept ornamentation to a minimum. Geometric borders were the most favoured options, but other influences had their day. Following Napoleon's campaign in Egypt (1798–1801), for example, otherwise plain empire-line dresses took on ancient Egyptian motifs (first seen on Josephine's dresses). Over the coming years these became increasingly elaborate – and decreasingly classical – as women tired of the unchanging minimalism of the empire-line shape. Gothic, medieval and Elizabethan influences were among the new developments.

Top: A model wearing a jersey empire-line dress from the Blanes A/W collection of 1962/63.
Left: Madame Raymond de Verninac, born Henriette Delacroix, sister of the artist Eugène Delacroix, painted in 1799.

During the first two decades of the nineteenth century, the empire line really was a predominantly French phenomenon. While French women found new embellishments to reinvigorate the style, English women soon abandoned it altogether, seeing their dress waistlines drop considerably. This, in part, stemmed from the unsuitability of the flimsy style to the British climate. One commentator, Lady Morgan, reported that, contrary to the empire line's seeming lightness and simplicity, she found it 'the most uncomfortable style of dress – so scanty that it was difficult to walk in them and to make them tighter still, invisible petticoats are worn'.

Indeed, prolonged war between what were then the two centres of European fashion – the UK and France – often affected their respective directions in matters of style. When peace was finally achieved in 1814, they began to share ideas on fashion – chiefly for the French to ridicule those of the English, and for the English to again start copying those of the French. Even French women soon began to give up on the high waistline however, with it reportedly dropping an inch a year until, by around 1825, the waistline was at the natural waist.

The empire line lived on; it was a key look among women in the USA during the 1890s, for example, and has been periodically revisited by such fashion houses as Yves Saint Laurent, partly due to how flattering it is on most body shapes. Perhaps it is most frequently seen on wedding dresses, with brides aiming to capture the classical elegance of Regency ladies, and on maternity dresses. Not for nothing did a piece of comic verse during the Regency period note that women 'all look as if they were got with child'.

Above: Actress Blake Lively wearing an empire-line dress while filming the US TV series *Gossip Girl* in New York in 2009.
Right: British actress Jacqueline Pearce in a grey and white striped maxi dress in 1968.

SHIFT DRESS

The story of the origins of the shift dress – a style that hangs straight from the shoulder without hugging the body's curves or cinching at the waist – is an entertaining one. Twenty-one-year-old New York socialite Lilly Pulitzer eloped with Peter Pulitzer and they moved to his Palm Beach home, where he also owned fruit groves. She decided to make fruit juices and sell them at the roadside, but asked her dressmaker to create a simple, inexpensive dress that she could happily get stained by the juice, and in a sufficiently bold pattern that it would hide it well anyway. The result was a sleeveless, knee-length, front-darted but otherwise minimalistically cut dress in loud patterns. The so-called 'Lilly' dress was not dissimilar to the straight-cut, low-waisted, embellished dresses worn by the rebellious, bob-haired and bust-flattening *garçonnes* or flappers from the mid-to-late 1920s. For them, as for the wearers of the 'Lilly' dress some 25 years on, such a silhouette suggested a progressive emancipation from fuss and clutter in dressmaking.

However, the dress's transition from roadside to fashion staple required friends in high places. The story has it that customers were as impressed by her dresses as her juices, so Pulitzer began to sell them too. But it took fashion barometer and school friend of Lilly Pulitzer, Jacqueline Kennedy – at the time the president's wife – to wear one on the cover of *Life* magazine, for the style to go mainstream. 'Jackie wore one of my dresses – it was made from kitchen curtain material – and people went crazy,' Pulitzer once recalled. 'Everybody loved them, and I went into the dress business.'

But, leading fashion designers would only be associated with the style from 1961, when Hubert de Givenchy created the costumes for Audrey Hepburn in *Breakfast at Tiffany's* (Blake Edwards), including a shift style based loosely on the waistless sack dresses he and others had

Opposite: The American socialite Wendy Vanderbilt and friend both wearing Lilly Pulitzer shift dresses in 1964.
Below left: American First Lady Jacqueline Kennedy in the Green Room at the White House in 1961.
Below right: American actress Mia Farrow on the set of *Rosemary's Baby* in 1967. Her much-copied short, layered hairstyle had just been cut by Vidal Sassoon.

introduced four years earlier. Hepburn's screen version came in black, but its sleek lines also represented modernity. And it certainly helped that Kennedy was also a customer of Givenchy.

In 1965, Yves Saint Laurent created one of the most widely recognized versions of the style with his wool jersey Mondrian dress, using the blank canvas of the shift dress to show geometric panels of strong colour, after Dutch artist Piet Mondrian's paintings. In the dress, Saint Laurent demonstrated a masterclass in dressmaking, setting in each block of jersey to create the semblance of Mondrian order and to accommodate the body imperceptibly, hiding all the shaping in the grid of the seams. In 1966, British designer Mary Quant created her minidress by shortening the shift dress in line with her miniskirts (see p.27). Leslie Hornby, aka Twiggy, took her first step to becoming the first internationally known model when she was hired to model the dress.

The uncomplicated nature and general ease of this understated dress ensured its reputation as a classic. A young Mia Farrow would make it something of a signature look, along with her boyish hairstyles also echoing the 1920s, although its appeal would peak after periods of more ostentatious fashion. Calvin Klein, for example, won praise for his shift dresses in the early 1990s after the excesses of the previous decade. Since a good fit was essential to the shift dress's appeal as it lacked distracting ornamentation, designer versions tended to be more complexly cut than outward appearances suggested: well-placed darts at the bust and a narrow A-line shape created a more flattering style.

Erin O'Connor wearing a simple black shift dress on the catwalk for Helmut Lang A/W 2001.

Piet Mondrian-inspired shift dress by French
designer Yves Saint Laurent in 1968.

HALTER-NECK DRESS

There was a very good reason why Joe DiMaggio, Marilyn Monroe's husband at the time, was said to have hated the cocktail dress she wore in Billy Wilder's 1955 movie *The Seven Year Itch.* for the famed scene when she stands on a subway grate and her dress billows up (see p.71). It was daringly revealing, to DiMaggio's chagrin: a halter-neck style, it not only enhanced the curvature of Monroe's breasts, but also left her shoulders and back bare. Designed by Oscar-winning costumier William Travilla, that dress became – thanks to the scene – an icon in its own right, later owned by actress Debbie Reynolds, and eventually sold at auction in 2011 for £2.8 million.

The halter-neck was created to tantalize, despite the term being derived from the halter placed around an animal's neck to effect better control of it. Dating from between 1914 and 1919, the neckline is credited to French designer Madeleine Vionnet – pioneer, too, of the bias cut, handkerchief dress and draped, Grecian-style dress. It is also said that she intentionally realized it in sensuous, streamlined, form-following fabrics such as crêpe de Chine and satin. Vionnet was arguably responsible for abandoning the constraints and silhouette imposed on women through the use of corsets; her halter-neck exposed the back but also varying degrees of cleavage, too. Her dresses expressed the natural female form. 'It was a pity to go against nature,' noted Vionnet, who went on to design a double halter-neck, with the front of the dress or swimsuit supported by two sets of straps fastened at the back of the neck.

During the boom years of the 1920s, the halter-neck dress became the sophisticated eveningwear of choice – and a risqué one, linking the style to notions of hedonism. While the neckline would later appear on swimsuits and casual tops, the halter-neck was, perhaps, the first 'come-hither' dress in an age in which any public sexual impropriety

Opposite: Hollywood 'bombshell' Jane Russell in a halter-neck dress in 1955.
Below left: Bianca Jagger and then husband Mick Jagger in New York in 1974.
Below right: A studio portrait of actress Barbara Stanwyck in 1910.

was social suicide. At first, only the superstars of the period – the likes of actress Clara Bow, who wore one for official studio portraits – could pull it off. Marlene Dietrich, Greta Garbo, Jean Harlow, Ginger Rogers and Katharine Hepburn all supported the style; Hepburn is even said to have inspired the halter-neck top that Levi's included in its 1938 'Tropical Togs' line of coloured denim. Furthermore, the halter-neck dress became the style of choice for a Hollywood facing the pre-war censorship of the Hays Code, which limited the amount of cleavage shown on screen; the back provided an alternative erogenous zone to reveal.

Synonymous with seductiveness and glamour during Hollywood's Golden Age, the halter-neck dress also became the signature style of another period that revelled in decadence: the 1970s. Sleek gowns by Roy Halston Frowick (better known simply as Halston) were particularly favoured during the disco era. The celebrity crowd, Bianca Jagger and Liza Minnelli, for example, made the Halston halter-neck a regular feature at New York's legendary bacchanalian Studio 54 nightclub.

Below left: Swedish model and actress Maud Adams in 1975.
Below right: Model wearing a cotton halter-neck in 1953.

A young Elizabeth Taylor shot for a studio portrait in 1955.

PRAIRIE DRESS

In 1967, everything changed for a company well established in Wales for making printed aprons and gardening smocks: Bernard and Laura Ashley produced their first dresses. They could not have been more different to the shapeless shift and short minidresses that then dominated the flesh-revealing fashion. Far from being modernistic, they obviously referenced the past; and they were demure rather than sexy. As Laura explained: 'I had to do something that was completely different because I knew in my heart that [the dominant fashion style of the 1960s] was not what most people wanted. I sensed that most people wanted to raise families, have gardens and live life as nicely as they can. They don't want to go out to nightclubs every night and get absolutely blotto.'

The Laura Ashley style hinted at a simpler, more innocent life, pretty rather than sassy. The dresses were a twist on Edwardian and Victorian patterns, characterized by a high neck with perhaps a stand-up or Peter Pan collar, pleated full-length skirt with maybe a flounce, long sleeves, puffs at the shoulder, button cuffs, sometimes button-fronted like a shirt, sometimes with a pin-tuck bodice. They were most appreciated for their distinctive, subtle prints, often floral or nature-inspired, but also with heraldic or medieval imagery. They were, in short, blends of all forms of historic romanticism, with later dresses exploring empire-line Regency style, too (see p.46).

The appeal of these blends of styles had much longevity. Sewing patterns for the look proliferated in a period when dressmaking was still a commonplace hobby; and when, as late as 1981, Lady Diana Spencer was first photographed as the girlfriend of Prince Charles, she was wearing a Laura Ashley dress. Although the glossier, power dressing of the 1980s would come to replace this soft-focus style, the Ashleys successfully implemented the nostalgic look of their dresses in homewares and interiors, becoming one of the first lifestyle brands.

The early success of Laura Ashley dresses in the UK reflected a wider cultural interest in the past: hugely successful television programmes of the time included *Upstairs Downstairs* and *The Forsyte Saga* (both set in the early 1900s). A similar nostalgia fuelled designers abroad: in 1974, the American television series *Little House on the Prairie* began its nine-year run, while the mid-1970s saw the advent of similarly romantic, homespun and home-made styles based on the history of the American Midwest pioneer.

Prairie, folk or granny dresses by such designers as Oscar de la Renta explored similar territory to those of Laura Ashley: ruffled and floor length, with pie-crust collars, feminine but covered up. By the late 1960s and early 1970s, the granny look was in, along with shawls, workman-like ankle boots and lace-trimmed petticoats. A number of designers, from Biba's Barbara Hulanicki to Bill Gibb and from Angela Gore to a more western-inspired Ralph Lauren were rifling through costume history books to offer their interpretation.

Top: A young Lady Diana Spencer in a Laura Ashley prairie dress, in Windsor in 1981.
Bottom: The ladies of the *Little House on the Prairie*, the hit US TV show that helped drive 'pioneer' fashion.
Opposite: A romantic, Edwardian-inspired bridal dress designed by Laura Ashley in 1986.

WRAP DRESS

Belgian-born Diane von Fürstenberg revived the idea of practicality and comfort in women's dressing without dispensing with femininity in the 1970s, much as American designer Claire McCardell had during the 1940s with her popover dress. 'Feel like a woman, wear a dress,' as von Fürstenberg put it in a 1973 advertisement. But not any dress. Her solution was a style of dress whose basic template was borrowed from those quintessentially comfortable garments the dressing gown and domestic housecoat, although the designer likened it more to such traditional forms of clothing as the kimono, toga or other garments without buttons or zips.

Von Fürstenberg's wrap dress did just what it said: it wrapped closely around the body, the fabric overlapping at the waist to fasten in a tie on the hip. Like Chanel's little black dress before it (see p.43), the wrap dress worked for all occasions, formal and casual, smart and alluring. It was, as von Fürstenberg put it, a 'very down-to-earth product, which was really a uniform. It felt very good. [It suited] all sorts of women ...young and old, fat and thin, poor and rich.'

The style was inspired less by von Fürstenberg's heroes Bill Blass and Diana Vreeland, than by seeing Julie Nixon Eisenhower, daughter of former US president Richard Nixon, on television wearing a wrap top with a wrap skirt. Von Fürstenberg's idea was to take the simplicity of the outfit a step further by making it a single, bright, boldly patterned cotton-jersey garment: a wrap dress. The style was launched in 1974. By 1975, von Fürstenberg was reported to be making 15,000 a week to keep up with demand; by the end of the following year, she had sold some four million of what had become a staple for both the Studio 54 high-glamour party goers and the well-to-do set of Park Avenue, New York, and beyond.

Opposite: Diane von Fürstenberg, fashion designer and pioneer of the wrap dress in 1973. Below: Actress Bérénice Marlohe in a scene from the 2012 James Bond film *Skyfall*.

As von Fürstenberg noted, it became 'an interesting cultural phenomenon. It's more than just a dress; it's a spirit.' In fact, the ethos of the dress – easy yet sassy – came to embody women's liberation in the 1970s, especially as more and more women entered the workplace and looked for an uncomplicated yet professional garment to wear. Von Fürstenberg was consequently cited in Dolly Parton's single 'Working Girl', while the wrap dress made women feel what they wanted to feel like: free and sexy, as the designer noted. Free was certainly one aspect; more personally for von Fürstenberg, the design of the dress came at the end of her marriage to Prince Egon of Fürstenberg, with the need to make an independent career for herself and have a hit to underpin it.

Certainly the press recognized that von Fürstenberg's one garment had made her 'the most marketable woman since Coco Chanel', as *Newsweek* put it in 1976. The wrap dress would have a second life during the 1990s, when its revival encouraged Von Furstenberg to relaunch the style in 1997.

Diane von Fürstenberg dresses from, **left**, 2004, **below**, 2002 and **opposite**, 2006.

SHIRT DRESS

The shirt dress, or shirtwaister, was the definitive style of the 1940s, less so for its fashionability than its easy utility. As the Woman's Institute of Domestic Arts and Sciences in the USA noted, the shirt dress was 'a simple, practical dress' that 'because of its trim simplicity and graceful dignity' was ideal for both classroom and in business. This was the button-down dress that helped adolescent girls feel more adult, and adult women feel ready to go anywhere. The style was worn as much for sport, golf especially, as for eveningwear. In its versatility it was, in some respects, the less glamorous forerunner of the little black dress (see p.42).

So uncomplicated was the style that it took interest from Christian Dior in 1947, with his seminal New Look breaking through post-war rationing and dowdiness, to make it fashionable. One dress, the 'Chérie', is said to epitomize the look: a soft silhouette with sloped shoulder, raised bustline, narrowed waist and full, lightly under-padded skirt – in Chérie's case, also heavily pleated. Such was Dior's affection for the shirt dress, it reappeared in collections for 1948 and 1949 too.

The shirt dress was now, as *Harper's Bazaar* called it, 'the essence of femininity'. As practical lifestyle magazine *Good Housekeeping* pointed out, at a time when magazines were notably powerful in influencing millions of women's clothing choices, Dior's prices were prohibitively high, but the template of narrow waist and full skirt that he had provided had great potential, especially if all those pleats were done away with and a more affordable, streamlined and easier-to-make look was created.

Small wonder then that the shirt dress became the signature style of stateside domesticity and motherhood, the uniform of that post-war invention of the American advertising industry: the housewife. Some – in large part due to influential US television shows of the period, most notably *Leave It to Beaver* – have even suggested that it helped define the woman's place as being in the home. Furthermore, some companies marketed the shirt dress as a 'house dress'. After all, 1957 saw the publication of Anne Fogarty's *Wife Dressing: The Fine Art of Being a Well-Dressed Wife (With Provocative Notes for the Patient Husband Who Pays the Bills)*.

Above: An A/W 1986/87 Laura Ashley shirt dress.
Right: Two women in their summer dresses in 1955, the one on the left opting for the then fashionable button-through shirt dress style.

The shirt dress had, however, taken a long journey to this point of ubiquity. Shirtwaisters had been worn in the early 1900s, and a book published in 1917 entitled *Patterns for Blouses and Dresses* talked of the 'mannish shirtwaist' as being 'a garment so designed to follow practically the same lines as those of a man's négligée shirt'. By the 1920s, its practicality saw it adopted for various uniforms, those of nurses and teachers, for example. Come the 1940s, World War II's widespread rationing of textiles saw the UK bring in a range of government-approved Utility Clothing, for which the unembellished form of the shirt dress, with square shoulders and a straight skirt, became a staple. Throughout the 1950s, the shirt dress persisted and was regularly updated by the fabric choice; in 1955, for example, it was, as *Harper's Bazaar* suggested, all about 'the shirtwaist in flower, its natural up-to-the-minute aptness made suddenly more so by one of spring's miraculous botanical prints – sharp acid greens and yellow and tart vermillion pinks that blaze.'

A long history may have ensured that the shirt dress became a style to which womenswear would repeatedly return, but the mid-1960s saw its first downturn in popularity, before, of course, it bounced back the next decade in sexier form thanks to Roy Halston Frowick and Ralph Lauren. Rudi Gernreich was one of the designers to help kill off the style; his 1967 show caused gasps when he surprised the audience of fashion buyers with a model wearing a belted shirt dress covering her knees, complete with nylon stockings, matching bag, shoes and gloves. Then out came another model in a thigh-revealing minidress in the same print as the shirtwaister. Gernreich called them 'Mrs Square and Miss Hip'. And, there was no doubt which was which.

Singer Taylor Swift in a more literal interpretation of a shirt dress, in Los Angeles in 2013.

KAFTAN

Call it what you will – from 'boubou' to 'takchita' and 'dashiki' as various cultures through history have – it is hard to conceive of a simpler or more ancient garment than the kaftan. Whether plain and unadorned, or boldly coloured, heavily decorated and panelled, as royalty and the well-off favoured, sometimes giving them as gifts to visiting dignitaries, the basic garment is essentially a fuss-free, loose, long-sleeved, three-quarter or ankle-length, over-the-head tunic. As such it preserved its wearer's dignity while keeping him or her cool.

The kaftan was historically a unisex garment, originating in the Middle East and Asia and popular with the Ottomans, who made them from velvet, silk brocade and metallic threads in indigo, red, violet and yellow. 'Kaftan' is a Persian word, with the first garments believed to have originated around 600BC in Mesopotamia – Syria, Kuwait, Iran, Iraq and Turkey (where, in Istanbul, the Topkapi Palace houses a collection of rare, historic and lavish kaftans).

Inevitably then, its take up as a fashion item was fuelled by a recurring interest in all things Eastern, exotic and mysterious. The kaftan appealed to the hippie movement of the 1960s, demonstrating an affinity with non-Western values. Elsewhere, fashion trendsetters such as *Vogue* editor Diana Vreeland – whose visit to Morocco had inspired a number of Eastern fashion editorials – quickly picked up on the style, too, as did major womenswear designers Pierre Cardin, Emilio Pucci, Krizia, Valentino and Oscar de la Renta, as well as such less well-known names as Germana Marucelli, Dorothée Bis and Thea Porter. Celebrities from Grace Kelly to Elizabeth Taylor wore the look.

For the designer, the kaftan, typically in wool, silk, cashmere or cotton, was as an ideal canvas for impressive displays of print and embellishment, an idea that remained into the 1970s. A departure from the basic kaftans picked up by the hippies for pennies in Eastern bazaars, more luxurious 'evening' versions, designed by Roy Halston Frowick, graced the celebrity set of New York's Studio 54 nightlife scene. Yves Saint Laurent – who had a home in Morocco, where he often found inspiration for his designs – was similarly enthused about the traditional garb's freedom, elegance and suggestion of bohemianism.

Yet this was not the first time the kaftan was in vogue: the marriage of Queen Victoria's granddaughter to Nicholas II of Russia at the end of the nineteenth century inspired a fleeting fashionability for the garment as she was photographed in a kaftan, a style then also worn by Russians. But this look to the East really came to a head in the 1910s, when Serge Diaghialev's Ballets Russes performed *Scheherazade*, with Eastern-inspired costumes by Léon Bakst. In turn, couturier Paul Poiret adopted the aesthetic of drapery, using his wife Denise as his model. Under his influence, the fitted, tightly waisted clothing typical of the period enjoyed a spell of the free and easy that reminded wearers of pre-Raphaelite painters and their muses, and was perfect for casual at-home entertaining. Indeed, it was this uncomplicated, flowing quality that ensured the kaftan would become a mainstay of summer dressing, in particular, at festivals, or as a more glamorous alternative to the sarong as beach or poolside attire.

Left: Jennifer Lopez wears a kaftan for the beach while shooting the video for 'Live It Up' in Florida in 2013.
Opposite: The French-born singer and actress Marie Laforêt, shot in the early 1970s.

A model posing in an A-line dress and
matching jacket by Bodin, with a hat by
Lanvin-Castillo, for the S/S 1962 collection.

A-LINE DRESS

Hemlines may rise and fall and certain styles have their moment, but few silhouettes can have been so influential in the late twentieth century as what came to be known as the A-line. The shape, triangular from the shoulders or hips, has historical precedent: sixteenth-century Elizabethan fashion insisted on the flattening of the bust and a full skirt, producing a proto-A-line shape; the hoops of underskirts in the seventeenth century created similar lines; and women's fashion during the Edwardian era, with its emphasis on such new physical pursuits as bicycle riding, teamed a blouse with an ankle-length flared skirt to also achieve an A-line effect. Even in the mid-twentieth century, designer Jacques Fath's swing coat of the late 1940s hinted at the A-line. But it was Christian Dior, who christened the style 'A-line' in his Spring collection of 1955.

Dior's was an exaggerated version: the key look was an unfussy, flared jacket over an even more flared pleated skirt, a true capital A, in keeping with the letter shapes that inspired his collections (he also produced styles based on H and Y). In fact, the A-line was devised in part to mark a distinct break with the nipped-in waist of his 'Corolle' line, introduced as part of the New Look in 1947, and influential for many years after. The A-line was, as *Vogue* quipped, 'the prettiest triangle since Pythagoras', and, although not immediately successful, it did inspire copies and sewing patterns.

It was in 1958, with Yves Saint Laurent's first collection at Christian Dior, that the A-line established itself as a truly modern shape with wide appeal, not least because it was distinctly flattering, narrowing the waist and hiding hips and thighs. Saint Laurent's 'Trapeze' collection offered knee-length coats and dresses that flared from the body more softly and less dramatically than Dior's designs, although more extreme takes were soon created by other designers.

Models line up in A-lines for designer André Courrèges's S/S 1968 collection.

In spite of its long history, the A-line, with its emphasis on comfort without sacrificing structure, came to be viewed as a futuristic shape, especially during the space age of the 1960s. The playfulness of the A line, Mary Quant-inspired minidress seemed especially suited to the boom in youth fashion over the decade. It was a graphic, wearable shape to which bold colours, patch pockets and various necklines could be applied. The A-line of the 1960s explored new fashion materials such as paper, PVC and other plastics; the fact that they could retain a stiffness made them ideal for the A-line, as French designers Pierre Cardin, Emanuel Ungaro and André Courrèges each investigated, the latter's 1964 'Moon Girl' collection including A-line minidresses in silver plastic inspired by astronaut suits. But, the A-line remained a fashion staple precisely because it worked regardless of length: come the 1970s, the A-line was appearing in longer styles, worn in denim with knee-high boots.

Below: Colourful A-line dresses by Hanae Mori and Charles Cooper modelled in 1970.
Opposite: A pale blue trapeze dress with welt seams by Claret from 1967.

PLEATED DRESS

The problem, from fashion's point of view, with the pleated skirt has been its long association with frumpiness. The pleated skirt bookends life either as a girl's kilt-like school uniform or the uniform of old age – the skirt of grandmotherly, dowdy Miss Marple figures, and Queen Elizabeth II when on less formal duties. The function of the pleats, allowing the cloth to attain an elasticity that encourages it to the cling to the body without the use of panels or darts, while also allowing ease of movement when required, has also made it unappealing to the less than svelte.

However, perhaps not so the pleated dress, which has moved beyond the utilitarian nature of the pleat to tap into what some have claimed is its youthful nature. In 1938, *The Montreal Gazette*, reporting on fashion out of New York, noted how 'no one can fail to be impressed with the way pleats have carried on – pleats for daytime and pleats for evening, pleated prints and pleated solid colors.... These pleated fashions have a young air that is irresistible.' In fact, curvy Marilyn Monroe provided one of the most famous moments in pleated dress history, when hers – designed by Hollywood costumier William Travilla – was lifted above her head in *The Seven Year Itch* (Billy Wilder, 1955).

Skirts and dresses alike with various kinds of pleating – among them knife, plissé, accordion, cartridge, box and Fortuny – have a long history going back to ancient Egypt and the Vikings. They were a common feature on the clothes of the wealthy (because pleating, of course, requires more fabric) during the medieval and Renaissance eras and well into the eighteenth century. They have also prompted innovative design history: the Fortuny pleat is named after Spanish designer Mariano Fortuny, whose secret pleat-setting process, developed for fine silks in 1907 and patented in 1909, allowed the creation of then revolutionary form-fitting dresses, including his floor-length, ancient-Greece-inspired 'Delphos', as worn by Lillian Gish and other movie stars of the silent screen.

Above: Dress, shirt and cape all from the A/W 1995/96 collection by Issey Miyake, the Japanese designer who made tight pleating the basis for an entire line.
Right: Régine Flory, dressed by Mariano Fortuny in Paris, c. 1910.

French sculptor-turned-designer Germains Krebs, better known as Madame Alix Grès, also won acclaim for her Grecian dresses during the late 1940s and 1950s, each dress comprising hand-stitched pleats of no more than 1mm width and so taking some 300 hours to intricately assemble. Pioneering American designer of casual wear Claire McCardell saw the accordion pleat's potential for less dressy clothing at about the same time, while in 1947 Christian Dior applied pleats to his 'Bar' suit with a skirt made from wool crêpe.

Pleats have invited a certain inventiveness: in the 1950s, Irish designer Sybil Connolly developed a process over eight months that allowed horizontal pleats to be permanently pressed into linen, aiming to make a feature of its tendency to crease anyway. 'Crumple it into a suitcase and it will emerge, uncrushed, uncrushable, to sweep grandly through a season of gaiety,' as *Vogue* noted in 1957. Some 8.2m (9 yards) of linen were required to make one pleated dress. And, in 1993, Japanese designer Issey Miyake launched his 'Pleats Please' line, based on using traditional tight pleating but in polyester fabrics to create lightweight and easy-to-wear modern garments, some of which also introduced zigzag pleating.

Throughout the twentieth century the pleated dress has drawn the attention of more progressive fashion designers, the likes of Elsa Schiaparelli, Jean Dessès and Yohji Yamamoto. But it is Miyake again, this time in the twenty-first century, who has arguably provided the most unexpected confluence of modern methodology with this ancient dressmaking technique: he used ultrasonic waves that emitted heat vibrations to create pleats of an intricacy not seen before for his 2004 'Fête' collection, particularly his 'Colombe' dress.

The poster for *The Seven Year Itch* (1955), featuring one of the most famous dresses in movie history.

4.

TROUSERS

leather trousers / palazzo pants / leggings / culottes /
jeans / hot pants / trouser suit / harem pants /
Capri pants / pajama pants

LEATHER TROUSERS

With their skintight fit, leather trousers are animalistic and sexually highly charged. That, of course, was not their original intention; a form of leather trousers has been worn as a protective leg covering since prehistoric times by, among others, the ancient Greeks, the Inuits and other peoples from extreme cold climates and the knights of medieval Europe who wore them as a layer between skin and armour, much as motorcyclists have worn them since the early twentieth century.

It was for much the same reason that, in the nineteenth century, they came to be associated with the ranchers of the American west, even if technically chaps – from the Spanish *chaperajos*, meaning 'leg of iron' – were seat-less and worn over the top of jeans to protect clothes while in the saddle. It was this aspect of leather trouser lore that inspired Jim Morrison of The Doors. He took his cue from *The Fugitive Kind* (Sidney Lumet, 1960), in which Marlon Brando plays a modern-day cowboy. Morrison persuaded a Beverly Hills tailor – a German immigrant trained in making traditional lederhosen – to make his not out of sturdy cow leather, but super-soft glove leather, which allowed the fit to be much more figure-hugging. This is how leather trousers attained their most famous association: as part of the uniform – typically in black or red – of the rock god, from Eddie Cochran to Gene Vincent and from the Beatles in their Hamburg residency years to the glam rock of Aerosmith, Mötley Crüe, Guns N' Roses and Kiss.

This more theatrical form of rock from the mid-1970s through to the mid-1980s, heightened the suggestiveness of leather trousers as signifiers of outsider cultures, rebelliousness and sex, rather than protection, and was embraced as much by women as by men. Early female rockers of the period, Suzi Quatro, Joan Jett, Chrissie Hynde, Tina Turner and Lita Ford in particular, led the way, perhaps seeing in leather trousers a way to be perceived as equal to their

Opposite: French actress and 'sex kitten' Brigitte Bardot in PVC jacket and leather trousers during the 1960s.
Below: American rock singer Suzi Quatro in black leather rock 'n' roll uniform, in 1973.

male contemporaries, and certainly distancing themselves from any stereotypical notions of soft-edged, pink femininity. Strutting rock god turned sassy rock chick.

It was not until designer versions of leather trousers emerged in parallel over the same period that the garment lost some of its grit in favour of glamour, in large part due to a reinstatement of femininity; the pants were teamed with contrasting stiletto heels or loose silk blouses. Leather has a natural give to it, but is also able to provide structure and definition, making it suitable for most women's body shapes. Out went the association with the louche, in came one with luxuriousness with an edgy coolness.

Claude Montana, the French designer who often referenced the fetishistic and macho, made leather trousers a key part of his first collection in 1977. Around the same time, Thierry Mugler also made them part of his signature style, in patent leather and stretch leathers for an even closer fit. Over the next 15 years or so the catwalk would see leather trousers undergo multiple variations: as hot pants, rhinestone-covered, in every colour from the neon (Versace) to the neutral (Calvin Klein) and, later, even as leggings. Thanks to designers such as Isabel Marant and Balmain, leather trousers became a popular alternative to skinny jeans.

Left: Chrissie Hynde, lead singer of The Pretenders, performing in the late 1970s.
Below: Singer Marianne Faithful in fur and black leather, at Shepperton Studios, UK, in 1967.
Opposite: Debbie Harry, lead singer of Blondie, in a studio shot taken in 1977.

PALAZZO PANTS

With their light fabric (often silk crêpe or jersey) and voluminous proportions, palazzo pants are long trousers with a loose and very wide leg that flares from the hip. It is perhaps little wonder that the grandly named palazzo pants – after the Italian for 'palace' – were originally known more prosaically as 'beach trousers'. After all, they allowed air to circulate against the skin without actually revealing any skin; they were skirt-like but would protect the wearer's modesty in case of a coastal breeze. This made the style ideal for the chic resorts defined and populated by the wealthy in the early decades of the twentieth century, as womenswear was freed by changing social values to embrace elements of the male wardrobe, such as trousers.

The trouser had obvious appeal: it was elegant, narrowed the waist and was comfortable. Sometimes it was worn with a loose matching top to create a more dramatic version of the look, obviously inspired by pyjamas. Examples of this style were produced in the 1920s by Parisian couturiers Edward Molyneux and Paul Poiret (who also made harem pants fashionable, see p.96). Furthermore, their comfort made palazzo pants a popular choice for lounging around the house – as such, they may represent the origins of leisurewear.

Coco Chanel was a fan, sporting them herself on vacation, but also taking them out of their usual summertime context by producing them in jersey wool for her shop in Deauville, Normandy. Chanel also liberated the breton top from the traditional garb of fishermen (see p.105) and palazzo pants may owe some debt to the wide-legged trousers worn by gondoliers in Venice.

Chanel was not the only woman who favoured palazzo pants: they were popular in similar forms with such actresses of Hollywood's Golden Age as Veronica Lake and Carole Lombard, who caught the headlines by wearing the style to play golf with her husband Clark Gable at Los Angeles's upmarket Riviera Country Club. Actress and progressive stylist Katharine Hepburn wore a similar style – more trouser-like and with a turn-up – a decade later, which she termed 'lounge pants'; and many women during the 1960s found them a means of wearing trousers without doing so in an obvious way that would offend a society that still believed trousers should only form part of the male wardrobe.

This was in no small part down to the palazzo collection produced in 1960 by influential aristocratic Russian-Georgian designer Irene Galitzine, whose silky, wide-legged trousers helped the palazzo style become a fixture of more avant-garde eveningwear dress at society events. It was *Vogue* editor Diana Vreeland who dubbed them 'palazzo pants', a nod to the expensive Mediterranean resorts for which they seemed ideal.

Fashion designer Coco Chanel with Duke Laurino of Rome at the Lido in the 1920s.

Palazzo pants were not for wallflowers. Their expanse of fabric soon became a site for experimentation in embroidery and bold prints. For example, Italian air-force-flyer-turned-designer and 'prince of prints', Emilio Pucci produced silk jersey pants with geometric, op-art-style, almost psychedelic, patterns during the 1960s. The trousers also lent themselves to the lightness of chiffon jersey, which Pucci invented in 1968.

Women had largely been liberated from strictures of dress by the 1970s when Bianca Jagger made palazzo pants her trademark and was widely emulated. Making a fashion comeback, the style was seen on Ingrid Bergman in 1975 when she attended The Oscars, and was considered elegant, yet edgy at a time when the dress code dictated traditional black tie or evening dress. Palazzo pants may have been historically associated with leisure and even sportswear, but their floaty silhouette and their suitability for fine-gauge fabrics make them ideal for eveningwear. Very feminine, elegant and available in multiple hues and prints, palazzo pants are kept in vogue by designers from Céline to Marc Jacobs.

A model wearing palazzo pants in heavy silk crêpe by Emilio Pucci in 1968.

LEGGINGS

When Olivia Newton-John appeared in the video for the song 'Physical' in 1981, she was aptly dressed for the song and for the decade's fascination with work-out routines: headband, cotton top knotted at the waist, leotard and leggings. During the decade she was not alone in borrowing this latter piece of dancer's attire: Madonna, Cindi Lauper and girl group Bananarama all sported them, wearing them often as a form of undergarment beneath a short skirt and sometimes with leg warmers.

Leggings may have been one of the styles that defined the late 1970s and 1980s, but, like their historic relation tights, their appeal was also in great part down to their comfort and ease of wear. The same thinking lay behind their sartorial antecedent, too. Despite bewilderment during the 2010s at the idea of men wearing 'meggings' (men's leggings), from the feudal 1300s on, leggings were worn by men as a protective layer. This initially comprised a two-piece garment – one sleeve for each leg – made of wool or leather and worn under chain mail by knights or a smock by those serfs who worked the land. Outdoorsmen of all kinds appreciated the protective leather-stocking layer such a garment afforded, and, ultimately, it was from it that long johns for men developed, and the likes of bloomers for women.

Audrey Hepburn made a form of leggings – worn in black, with ballet pumps and a white shirt or black polo neck – something of a signature look after appearing in them in *Funny Face* (Stanley Donen, 1957), a musical film with a plot in part about the search for the next big fashion trend by a photographer character loosely based on Richard Avedon. But, it was not until two years later that a true second-skin, trouser-like garment was developed for women, when, for the first time, advances in textile technology made stretch materials that held their shape and elasticity a possibility.

A model in abstract patterned leggings by designer Maya Hansen, in Madrid in 2002.

Chemical company DuPont invented the first versions of Lycra in 1959, with claims that its spandex fibres could stretch up to 500 per cent while retaining shape. This led to the creation of super-skinny, fabric-belted trousers akin to the Capri pants popular at the time (see p.98), while the world of dance soon picked up on similar styles, both for their flexibility and their means of keeping the leg muscles warm during rehearsal.

It was just a short leap from professional to amateur use, with the late 1970s seeing leggings become a regular at roller discos. They were a staple during the dance and aerobics boom of the 1980s – driven by *Jane Fonda's Workout Book* (1982) and *Flashdance* (Adrian Lyne, 1983) – at the same time as designers embraced them as fashionable. Perhaps the most important among these was New York designer Norma Kamali, whose sweats collection first took workout gear from the studio to the street, with London designers David Holah and Stevie Stewart's Bodymap label, launched in 1982, doing much to give leggings a stylistic edge.

American actress Debbie Reynolds practising
a dance routine in black leggings and heels.

CULOTTES

When Italian designer Elsa Schiaparelli wore what appeared to be a divided skirt in London on a trip to buy tweeds in spring of 1931, it caused a sensation. While trousers on all but the most progressive (or famous) of women were considered disrespectful, women had worn what amounted to a hybrid shorts/trousers/skirt garment since the mid-1920s, ostensibly to better allow them to take part in the various sports and physical activities that were becoming fashionable.

However, this hybrid had always been hidden under some semblance of a wrap-around skirt, if only to keep up appearances of standard feminine dress. The garment induced a form of mass self-delusion: as long as the shorts-trousers could pass for a skirt, society would turn a blind eye to the breach of form. Schiaparelli did away with that, and was condemned by the British press. Tennis player Lilí de Álvarez, who wore Schiaparelli's 'divided skirt' for the Wimbledon tournament in the same year, was also criticized.

One theory has it that the culotte was out of favour following the obscenity trial of British author Radclyffe Hall for her 1928 novel *The Well of Loneliness* about a 'sexual invert'. Before the trial, women who chose to wear trousers were, in the UK at least, considered merely affected oddballs, but afterwards they were associated with lesbianism. The heat was less intense among the fashion followers of France, for whom the style was historically familiar. There, something like the Schiaparelli garment had been worn by aristocratic gentlemen since the 1500s. Culottes, in fact, came to be better known because of the opposition to them: during the 1790s and the French Revolution, those against the rigidly hierarchical system dubbed themselves the 'sans-culottes' (and their anti-elitist philosophy 'sans-culottism') or 'without breeches', and distinguished themselves by dressing in full-length trousers.

Culottes slowly achieved acceptance, in part for their novelty. In 1939 the *Deseret News* reported that 'Schiaparelli's flair for leading off with something entirely new and fun to wear must be responsible for her terrific popularity. Witness the tailleur, for example, with its divided skirt – or "jupe culotte", bloused like old-fashioned "gym" bloomers – in place of the regulation skirt.' Yet, the peak in interest for culottes did not come until the 1950s.

The brief popularity of gauchos, a trouser modelled on those worn by the South American cowboys of the same name, was partly to thank for this peak. Worn to mid-calf length, and definitely a form of trouser, they were a gentler reintroduction to the similar but shorter culottes, by then typically worn to the knee or, daringly, the mid-thigh. While culottes would make occasional returns to fashion over the following decades – such designers as Stella McCartney, Marc Jacobs and Bottega Veneta proposed them again in 2011, for example – they more often than not divide opinion, appropriately enough, their very halfway-house status limiting their appeal.

| A 'divided skirt', worn by more progressive women for the hunting season of 1922.

Above: Blue knee-length culottes shots for *Vogue* in 1955.
Right: Fashion designer Elsa Schiaparelli, pioneer of culottes for women, in London in the 1920s.

JEANS

Actress Brooke Shields was just 15 when she appeared in a television advert for Calvin Klein jeans in 1980. Her age might not have provoked the controversy that followed were it not for the way the ad lingered over her writhing body and the tag line that accompanied the vision: 'You wanna know what comes between me and my Calvins? Nothing.' It was enough to prompt Women Against Violence in Pornography and the Media, a USA campaign group, to condemn the ad as nothing more than 'using children in sexually enticing postures to sell a product'.

It was also enough to turn Calvin Klein from a $25m company into a $180m company in under a year. It was, as brands such as Gloria Vanderbilt, Fiorucci and Jordache would capitalize on, the realization of the 'designer denim' market. The message was not just that sex sells, but that jeans were sexy – an idea that ad agency Bartle Bogle Hegarty would explore in its mid-1980s 'Launderette' and 'Bath' television ads, featuring buff men in Levi's 501s in various states of undress.

The 1970s and 1980s saw the feminization of five-pocket western jeans, until then largely associated with the manly pursuits for which Levi Strauss and Jacob W. Davis (the inventor of copper rivets to strengthen stress points) had devised the garment in 1873 – the work of miners, cowboys and, later, industrial workers. However, Levi's designed its first pair of jeans exclusively for women in 1934. Lady Levi's, lot number 701, were created primarily for women working on ranches, although a picture appeared in *Vogue* in 1935. The zip fly was first introduced in this style in 1947 for those who considered the button fly inappropriate for women.

Jeans have come a long way and are available in various fits and finishes, from skinny to carpenter and from sandblasted to stonewashed. Here is a garment made of a fabric first woven in Nîmes, France (hence,

**Opposite: Marilyn Monroe in denim jacket and jeans in 1960 on the set of *The Misfits*.
Below: American actress Brooke Shields posing in an advertisement for Calvin Klein Jeans shot by Richard Avedon in 1980.**

Calvin Klein Jeans

'de Nîmes' or 'denim') and worn since the seventeenth century by the merchant sailors of Genoa (from which comes the term 'jeans').

In the 1940s, groundbreaking American ready-to-wear designer Claire McCardell – creator of the 'popover' dress that wrapped around the body and the shirtwaister, see p.59 – was one of the first to apply the durability of denim to womenswear, with a view to dressing a new, active, fast-living post-war woman with her collection of casual, sporty, functional clothes. This gave denim its first cachet among East Coast white-collar professionals, and gave the first hint that jeans could be more than the uniform of the teenager and be worn by sophisticated adults not going to a country-and-western hoedown.

However, when Marilyn Monroe wore 501s in *The Misfits* (John Huston, 1961) it was in contrast to her obviously feminine glamour. The countercultural American West Coast hippies of the mid-to-late 1960s, together with campaigners for peace and equal rights, wore them for practicality – they were cheap, plentiful and comfortable – as a statement of equality, to show community and blue-collar 'everyman' solidarity, but also, crucially, to undercut gender stereotypes. That changed when Calvin Klein became the first fashion designer to show jeans on the catwalk, in 1976, although it would not be until 1981 that Levi's launched 501s specifically for women.

These were major steps in the appropriation of jeans by women's fashion. A myriad of styles came on the market, from boot-cut jeans (devised as the 'cowboy cut' by Wrangler back in 1947) to straight, baggy, 'boyfriend-cut' jeans (an echo of the fact that if a woman wanted to wear jeans prior to fashion's interest in the garment, she would have to borrow her boyfriend's) and the low-rise jeans that followed designer Alexander McQueen's 1993 'bumsters'.

Below left: A model for the Neiman Marcus department store in denim trousers by Claire McCardell, during the 1940s.
Below right: A model in customized Stars And Stripes jeans, New York, 2009.
Opposite: Stonewash skinny jeans from 2009.

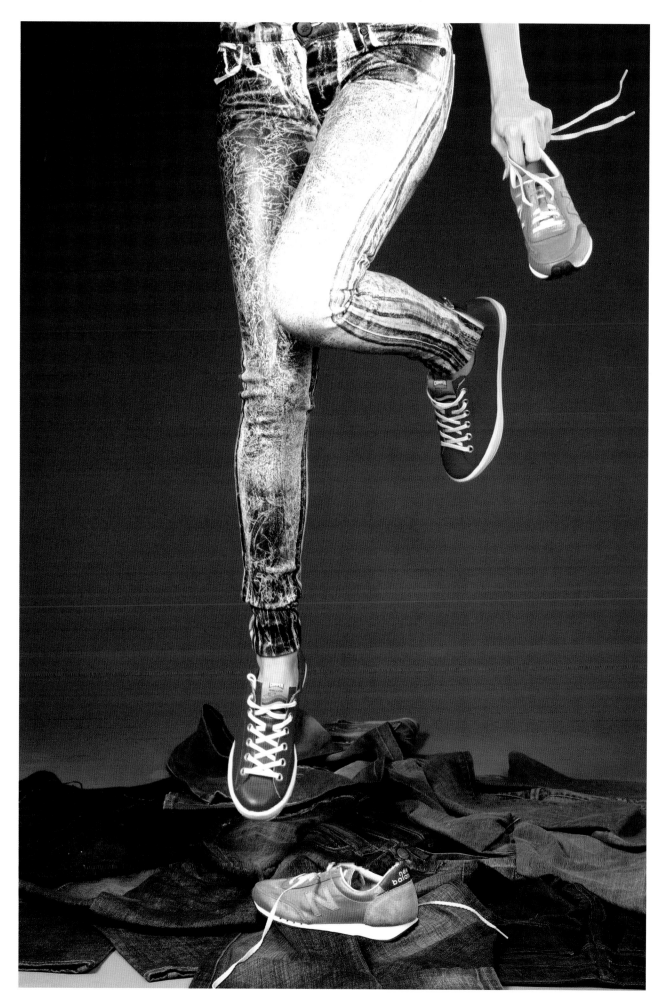

HOT PANTS

A very brief and usually tight-fitting short, hot pants are aptly named, both for their sexual connotations and for the intensity with which their moment in fashion flared up and then subsided. Few other womenswear garments were such an expression of their time, specifically 1971, a period of women's increased sexual liberation (and a concomitant conservative disapproval), of the rise of disco and even of the need to find a more practical, less revealing alternative to Mary Quant's revolutionary miniskirt (see p.27). Their invention, in fact, is also attributed to Quant, their name to *Women's Wear Daily*. By the end of 1971, *Life* magazine summed up the year sartorially, declaring, 'hot pants: a short but happy career'.

Hot pants epitomized the decade's growing daring in women's fashion. They were a shorter version of the fitted, beach-party shorts popular during the 1940s and 1950s, notably on Betty Grable, Marilyn Monroe, Esther Williams and on the illustrated pin-ups by George Petty and Alberto Vargas. They also questioned how that daring might cross a culturally acceptable line about propriety and how much flesh a woman could or should reveal.

One minute hot pants were high fashion, introduced on the catwalks of France and Italy for the 1970/71 Autumn/Winter collection, the next they were a mass-market item worn to parties, weddings and offices. Most famously, the airline stewardesses of Southwest Airlines in the USA wore orange hot pants and go-go boots as part of their uniform. Another reason why 1971 was a boom time for hot pants was due to an advance in fabric technology: the creation of polyester, which allowed the shorts to be stretchy and close fitting. The style inspired endless sewing patterns, new tequila and schnapps cocktails and songs from Vicki Anderson, Soul Brothers Inc., Bobby Byrd and James Brown. In 'Hot Pants' (1971), Brown sang: 'Hot pants make you sure of yourself/Good Lord – you walk like you got the only loving left', which also identified the style as ideal to dance in.

Opposite: A model on the catwalk in tan leather hotpants by John Galliano for the Christian Dior Summer 2000 collection.
Below: Jennifer Lopez on the set of a video shoot in 2002.
Right: 'I'm Cheryl. Fly me.' Stewardesses for Southwest Airlines of Texas in their uniform of leather boots and hot pants in accordance with the airline's motto that 'sex sells seats', during the early 1970s.

There were those who condemned hot pants as symbolic of sexual availability and the uniform of dubious cocktail waitresses, strippers and prostitutes. These were exactly the kind of cultural export non-Western countries did not want, not even in satin or crushed velvet, let alone in the flesh tones that, from a distance, suggested the wearer was semi-naked. Hot pants were denounced by Daniel Moi, vice-president of Kenya, as an 'undesirable and unbecoming kind of grotesque dress'. Even the West recognized the double life of hot pants: when the costume department for the movie *Taxi Driver* (Martin Scorsese, 1976) wanted to express the lost innocence of Jodie Foster's Iris when she turned child prostitute, it said it with hot pants.

This – and the rapid shift in fashion towards longer skirt styles – was the kind of association that tolled the knell for such short shorts. Think of the denim cut-offs worn by Daisy Duke in *The Dukes of Hazzard* (a long-running US television series beginning in 1979) or the fur and suede pair in the Fashion Institute of Technology collection in New York for a sense of how the style – although periodically resurrected by designers Katharine Hamnett, Azzedine Alaïa and Dolce & Gabbana, and performers such as Kylie Minogue in her gold lamé hot pants and Beyoncé in black leather ones – belongs to the 1970s, along with platform boots and flares.

Left: American actress Jodie Foster on the set of *Taxi Driver* (1976).
Below: Japanese artist Yoko Ono at a gallery opening during the 1970s.
Opposite: Italian actress Sophia Loren, posing for a publicity shot, in Rome, 1955.

TROUSER SUIT

It was bold for any woman to play with gender stereotypes through her clothing during the 1920s and 1930s. Exceptions, perhaps, were the Hollywood stars such as Marlene Dietrich, who wore trouser suits by Elsa Schiaparelli, and Josephine Baker, a regular at the Parisian men's bespoke tailor Cifonelli, or later such artists as Frida Kahlo and Lee Miller. Their celebrity and/or avant-garde lifestyle somehow permitted it. But not for others.

Society has long-held deeply cultural prohibitions against women dressing as men, sometimes, as in the late eighteenth and early nineteenth centuries, even proscribing it in law. It was only from the early 1890s through to late in the first decade of the 1900s that women were permitted to wear trousers in public for horse riding and bicycle riding. This was not, however, an issue for most women, and fewer still would have considered wearing what was strongly defined as a man's two-piece suit – it was the choice of some early women's rights campaigners during the 1920s precisely because of its scandalous nature and bohemianism.

This was political dressing, much as, historically, other women saw the power benefits of male dress and adopted these psychological advantages full-time. In the mid-nineteenth century, Josephine Monaghan was forced west in America's frontier land after having an illegitimate child, and survived by dressing as a man, cropping her hair and even scarring her face for full effect. Portuguese general Tito Gomes was jailed for three years in the 1990s after fraudulently collecting a military pension for twenty years. The general, better known to her family as Maria Teresinha Gomes, said that one day she had put on the uniform for a carnival and noticed how 'everyone respected me, while as a women I felt diminished'. Women pirates from the early 1700s Anne Bonny and Mary Read through to jazz musician Billy Tipton in the 1900s all found they were awarded privileges dressed as men that they never gained as women.

In contrast, up until World War II, most women who did wear trousers did so purely for acceptable reasons of practicality – for ranch or factory work, or because one happened to be an adventurer–aviator like Amelia Earhart. But this was a trend that the war made much more commonplace, so much so that throughout the 1940s it became fashionable for women to wear trousers, again assisted by the endorsement of 'slacks' by Hollywood stars such as Katharine Hepburn (whose characters often played on her supposed mannishness). Trousers were worn for sport and leisure. For most, the tailored suit, however, remained an outsider proposition – the stuff of theatre and androgynous play. It was a perception that would last, as shown by Julie Andrews in *Victor/Victoria* (Blake Edwards, 1982), Annie Lennox of the Eurythmics and Madonna during her 'Vogue' era.

Opposite: Singers Serge Gainsbourg and Jane Birkin wearing matching Cerruti suits at their Paris apartment in 1969.
Left: A trouser suit with cropped jacket in a Prince of Wales check by Yves Saint Laurent for the Summer 1997 collection.

What type of suit would become accepted by society and fashion alike? It turned out to be a much softer, more feminine version, popularized by André Courrèges and Yves Saint Laurent in the mid-1960s. Most noteworthy was the latter's 'Le Smoking' of 1966, a velvet and wool dinner suit reinterpreted for the female physique, which helped revolutionize attitudes towards women in trousers and scandalized society in the process. When singer Françoise Hardy wore it to the Paris Opera, 'people screamed and hollered', she recalled. New York socialite Nan Kempner was refused entry to upmarket restaurant La Côte Basque in 1968 wearing a trouser suit, so she removed the trousers and wore the jacket alone as a kind of impromptu minidress (and was admitted). 'For a woman, Le Smoking is an indispensable garment with which she finds herself continually in fashion, because it is about style, not fashion. Fashions come and go but style is forever,' as Saint Laurent noted in 2005.

Through the 1970s, the pant suit was taken on by American designers Ralph Lauren, Bill Blass and Calvin Klein. The fabrics used may have been traditionally masculine – flannel and tweed – but the cut was more fitted in the body, looser in the leg and altogether less manly. By the end of the decade, and in no small part thanks to the wardrobe of Diane Keaton in Woody Allen's *Annie Hall* (1977), women wearing what a few decades before had been considered masculine clothing was now mainstream. Come the 1980s, and power dressing, the trouser suit complemented the corporate climb of women in the workplace, even somehow symbolizing the idea of playing businessmen at their own game.

Below left: A be-suited Jane Birkin in 1982.
Below right: German-born actress Marlene Dietrich during the 1920s – her roles allowed her to challenge gender-based conventions of dress.
Opposite: Bianca Jagger wears a double-breasted white suit in London in 1979.

HAREM PANTS

If fashion was, during the nineteenth and twentieth centuries, mostly forged in the West, that has only inspired a fascination with the traditional attire of the East. The kaftan (see p.64) or cocoon coat, for example, both derive from a curiosity with the Orient, and the same can be said of harem pants, as they perhaps pejoratively came to be known. In fact, the voluminous, drop-crotch style of the historically unisex trouser, characteristically tight in the leg from the calf down or at the ankle, dates back to Asia some two thousand years ago, where, depending on the region, they went by some variation on the name *shalvaar*. This is a Persian word meaning 'trousers' and the Persians lay claim to having invented the garment in its basic form.

Then, women might have worn the style as a means of safeguarding their sexuality in a patriarchal society; the very shapelessness of harem pants disguised any feminine form beneath. Today, the style is still worn throughout the Middle East, though more as a traditional form of loungewear, notwithstanding its association with rapper MC Hammer, whose 1990 video for 'U Can't Touch This' might be credited with reintroducing the similar parachute-pant style to the West and giving it a brief pop-culture currency.

The transition of harem pants from East to West is more accurately attributed to Amelia Jenks Bloomer, an American of the nineteenth century who first suggested, in a feminist publication called *The Lily*, that women give up their petticoats in favour of the advantages of a two-legged garment worn – for its ease and comfort – by Turkish women. 'Turkish trousers' soon took on their proponent's name – bloomers – and were worn as a symbol of female emancipation (perhaps with some irony, given their original role). Generally considered too radical a move away from perceived notions of proper women's dress, they did not catch on with the wider public until after Bloomer's death in 1895, and then in large part because of the popularity of the new leisure pursuit of bicycling.

Even when, in 1909, French couturier Paul Poiret first attempted to give bloomers, or harem pants, a fashion spin, they failed to ignite much interest beyond their practical use for playing sports. And, this was in spite of him designing them in such proportions that they looked more skirt- than trouser-like. He even threw a 'Thousand and Second Night' party set in a fantastical version of the East, playing on the contemporary fascination with Orientalism in France, partly due to a new hit translation of *The Thousand and One Nights*. For women to wear any form of trouser was generally deemed an affront to the social order, so bloomers only became part of the mainstream everyday wardrobe as undergarments.

It was not until the mid-1960s and early 1970s – with another exploration of exotic cultures in the West – that harem pants became an established style for women, again as part of a broader appropriation of Eastern dress that included turbans and tunics. Issey Miyake and Yves Saint Laurent were among those designers leading the way, the latter particularly when he teamed harem pants with heels to give a new option for eveningwear. Ralph Lauren revisited the style in 2009

Left: A 1920s fashion illustration of black satin crêpe harem pants and crêpe de Chine top by Edward Molyneux.
Opposite: Harem pants in 'Desert Fox' photo shoot by Patrick Demarchelier for *Vogue*, 2009.

CAPRI PANTS

Capri may have been an unlikely inspiration for a fashion designer whose first studio and store, Salon Sonja, opened in the grim surroundings of Munich in 1945 in the immediate aftermath of World War II. But it was there that Prussian designer Sonja de Lennart devised the two key pieces of what she would call her 'Capri' collection, named simply after her favourite holiday destination: a wide skirt with matching wide belt and a blouse with three-quarter-length sleeves. Three years later when women, or at least those women who wore trousers, were still sporting wide, straight-legged styles, she added to the collection with a trouser that was slim cut and cropped just above the ankle (or shorter for her summer version), with a small split along the seam. Naturally enough, she named them Capri pants.

'I was just hot,' de Lennart once told the *Bild* newspaper to explain the idea. 'I was with my parents on Capri, cut my long trousers and strode through the water. That was wonderful. I found that these pants should be able to work anywhere.'

They seemed decidedly modern – streamlined, svelte and fitted – at a time when people wanted especially to look forward. German actress Mady Rahl took up the style, which helped to create local demand, but it was Hollywood, where more influential leading ladies embraced Capri pants, that they became a signature style of the 1950s. This was the time when de Lennart also combined her designs to show the trousers worn under a button-through Capri skirt. Audrey Hepburn, under costumier Edith Head's direction, wore de Lennart's Capri skirt, belt and blouse in *Roman Holiday* (William Wyler, 1953), and she would wear the pants, teamed with kitten heels (see p.176), and remade by Hubert de Givenchy from de Lennart's pattern, in both *Sabrina* (Billy Wilder, 1954) and *Funny Face* (Stanley Donen, 1957), making them a key component of her own style.

Following Hepburn, other stars wore the style, too, appropriately enough, given that Capri had become a holiday destination for the rich and famous. The style seemed to ably bridge the gap between those whose image was one of seductiveness – Jane Russell, Ava Gardner, Sophia Loren, Brigitte Bardot, Marilyn Monroe and Elizabeth Taylor – and those whose image was more family-friendly and comedic – Doris Day and Mary Tyler Moore, for example. That said, in her role as Laura Petrie in the hit early 1960s USA television series *The Dick Van Dyke Show*, Moore often wore tight Capri pants, which caused some controversy. Most housewives of the era wore dresses, at least on television. Moore countered that most housewives she knew wore trousers, and insisted that she did.

Other designers soon produced their own versions, cropped mid-calf, for example, or cuffed just below the knee as so-called 'pedal pushers' or 'clamdiggers', or even longer, as cigarette trousers. Customers had come to appreciate the style's versatility, looking just as good with heels as with ballet pumps.

Top: Swedish actress Anita Ekberg – of *La Dolce Vita* fame – in cream Capri pants for a publicity shoot in Hollywood during the 1960s.
Left: Street-style shot of a floral Capri pant-clad visitor to London Fashion Week 2012.

The poster for *Funny Face* (1957) featuring Audrey Hepburn as bookish Francophile-turned-model – her black Capri pants were shorthand for intellectual Parisian chic.

PAJAMA PANTS

There was, in underwear becoming outerwear in the 1980s and '90s, a certain decadence. But fashion had been there before, with nightwear becoming daywear. The palazzo pants Coco Chanel designed in the 1930s were similar to pyjama bottoms. And the loose trousers Katharine Hepburn would wear the following decade – seductively referred to as 'lounge pants' – also owed a debt to pyjamas. Indeed, 'pajama pants' was another term commonly used to describe such wide-leg trousers, whether they were plain and silky smooth, or boldly patterned in almost psychedelic swirls, (although later the term would be applied to more fitted, typically high-sheen and patterned trousers, sometimes worn with matching shirt).

Loose-fitting trousers had obvious appeal for women – they were elegant, narrowed the waist and, as men had discovered long before, they had the advantage of comfort. While the original pyjama – which can be traced back to the Persian 'payjama', meaning 'leg garment' in Hindustani – would not have been considered a night-time garment, British men in seventeenth-century India would wear them whenever they were relaxing. It was later in the nineteenth-century colonial period of the British in India, that pyjamas became fashionable with men back in the West as a garment to be worn in bed, sometimes with matching jacket. Although pyjamas were typically worn with bare feet, tailors would sometimes make them for their customers with a kind of sock in the same fabric sewn on. By the post-war twentieth-century period, pyjamas had become nightwear for women too, as demonstrated by Lucille Ball in the US TV series *I Love Lucy* and the Pink Ladies in *Grease* (Randal Kleiser, 1978, but set in the 1950s), who enjoyed gathering for pyjama parties.

But the comfort of pyjamas was too appealing to leave to one's sleep and as people began to adopt them before bedtime, pyjama trousers moved towards style alone. While ground-breaking couturiers such as Paul Poiret and Edward Molyneaux had, earlier on in the century, been the first to dress up the pyjama trouser in more luxe fabrics and trimmings to introduce them as suitable for eveningwear, only those in circles for whom such loose, freeing styles on women were acceptable, could wear them then. Later designers such as Yves Saint Laurent, Halston and Celine, who all appreciated the style's silky allure, would take up the idea and give it greater appeal. Then, come the 2010s, the likes of designers Diane von Fürstenberg, Louis Vuitton, Ferragamo and Tommy Hilfiger would revive pyjamas once more as both day- and eveningwear – only this time both matching top and bottom were worn, the trousers often more akin to printed silky cigarette pants than the loose versions that had gone before. Designer Stella McCartney perhaps took the style to its logical dressed-up conclusion: the three-piece pyjama suit.

Top: A pajama-pant outfit from the Halston 'Signature' collection for 2002.
Left: The bold graphic style of Pucci is given a large canvas with this bat-wing top and pajama pants during the 1960s.
Opposite: Pajama suit – complete with drawstring – by Giorgio Armani for the Resort collection 2008.

5.

TOPS

Breton top / blouse / twinset / crop top / T-shirt / tube top

BRETON TOP

Jean Seberg wore one in *À bout de souffle* (*Breathless*, Jean-Luc Godard, 1960), Jeanne Moreau made it a staple and Brigitte Bardot teamed hers with cropped jeans and ballet pumps to define a signature look. But, it was not just actresses in France who took to such a characteristically French garment as the Breton top. Kim Novak regularly wore a Breton, as did Natalie Wood, Edie Sedgwick, Audrey Hepburn – notably in *Funny Face* (Stanley Donen, 1957) – Marilyn Monroe and Jacqueline Kennedy Onassis.

The design of the *marinière*, as the French call it, was codified by an act of government on 27 March 1858, making it part of the official uniform of the French naval seaman (later copied by the Russian Navy). In actual fact, a variation of the *matelot* – as the top was also known, after the basic ranks of French seamen – had long been worn by the fishermen of Brittany. According to France's Musée National de la Marine, the *matelot* was characterized by some 22 alternate blue and white stripes, each said to mark one of Napoleon's victories.

Inspiration came to Gabrielle 'Coco' Chanel in 1913 when, the story goes, she was on holiday in Deauville, a seaside resort then regarded as extremely fashionable. She saw the simple striped tops, typically in white and navy or French blue, with boat necks and often cropped sleeves, worn by local sailors. Her fashion-house version made its first appearance as part of a broadly nautical-inspired collection in 1917. In keeping with her design philosophy of reinventing the comfort and practicality of menswear for newly liberated women, Chanel borrowed the Breton's look and made it stylish for the upper classes who, during the early decades of the twentieth century, could afford to follow fashion. Its nautical roots played to their ideas of Riviera seaside holiday attire, and Chanel intended it to be worn with wide-legged trousers. By the end of the 1930s, the Breton stripe for women had been elevated to haute-couture status.

Opposite: Brigitte Bardot playing the French card at the Cannes Film Festival in 1956.
Below left: American actress Kim Novak also playing the French card at the Cannes Film Festival in 1956.
Below right: British TV presenter Alexa Chung pairs the Breton with a flight jacket.

Throughout the twentieth century, the Breton's distinctly Gallic look would only be underlined by its adoption by French cultural luminaries from Françoise Sagan to Jean-Paul Sartre, such that it became an internationally recognized shorthand (and perhaps cliché) for French style. When costume designer Edith Head planned the clothing for Cary Grant's French Resistance leader turned cat burglar character in *To Catch a Thief* (Alfred Hitchcock, 1955), she chose for him a Breton.

No doubt assisted by fashion versions by the likes of Balmain and Gucci, the *marinière* became a distinctly unisex garment, worn as much by women as by men. Few garments from the male wardrobe, let alone ones with a military origin, have so successfully become a classic of womenswear, by turn gamine, simple and off-the-shoulder sexy. It would become, as Saint James, makers of the Breton top since 1889, put it, 'as classic as the little black dress'.

Below: Models wearing the latest Breton-inspired beach fashions in Florida in 1950. Opposite: The Breton stars in this Terence Donovan shoot with Karen Mulder for *Vogue* in 1991.

BLOUSE

From poet to peasant and from pussycat bow to folk and Edwardian, the blouse has been a constant fixture of the woman's wardrobe since the 1890s, before which the corset and full-length dress had been dominant for some centuries. The blouse was a product of women's move into the workforce; worn with a plain skirt, it provided the right balance of formality and comfort for the new office class. Indeed, such was their quick ubiquity that they attained a certain fashionability – either heavily embroidered in a way that had previously been the preserve of underwear or tucked and pleated to enhance the female form.

American illustrator Charles Gibson's idea of the modern woman, the 'Gibson Girl', with hair piled high on top of the head and wearing a crisp, white, button-front, fitted blouse, became a new standard of dress for progressive women. While the blouse often showed detailing characteristic of the Edwardian period, for example, a high neckline, lace edging and leg-of-mutton sleeves, it was fairly minimalistic compared with what had gone before. The blouse was ideal for increasingly emancipated, professional and active young woman, especially those who embraced new crazes such as bicycling. It remained, however, resolutely buttoned up.

When a brief vogue for a blouse with a V-neck or semi-transparent yoke at the front or back came in, it was denounced, both as indecorous and as a threat to the wearer's health, being dubbed the 'pneumonia blouse'. One organization in Massachusetts, the Purity Brigade, decided that the style was 'immodest', and they appealed to the community at large to abstain from encouraging such 'open work' effects. As *The Evening Post* reported in 1906: 'Strange to say, this movement, which was held up to ridicule at first, has continued for a year.... [But such is the fashionability of the blouse that] it is said that "looking from a skyscraper building today you can see mile upon mile of moving streams of white shirt waists".'

Opposite: Film director Sofia Coppola wearing a blouse with a Peter Pan collar in 2013.
Below left: Fashion illustration by De Losques for the French periodical *Les Modes* featuring typical Edwardian fashion of lace blouse, suit and hat.
Below right: A model wearing a blouse with dramatic over-sized bow in 1969.

Gary Cooper and Audrey Hepburn on location in Paris in 1957 during the filming of *Love in the Afternoon*.

Over the following decades, the blouse became more streamlined, fitted and, as the Purity Brigade might have found it, revealing. Necklines, sleeve and body lengths rose and fell with the fashion, but popularity remained constant. Worn with trousers, the blouse, sometimes short-sleeved, often more shirt-like, became a staple of 1940s and early 1950s dress, as epitomized by Katharine Hepburn. It would not, however, be until the 1970s, that the groundbreaking Edwardian look made a return, in keeping with the nostalgic romanticism that underpinned designs by the likes of Laura Ashley. Together with pearl strings, navy blazers and waxed jackets, it would be a key part of the influential look of the British upper-middle-class conservative style, termed 'Sloane Ranger', by cultural commentator Peter York. Designer versions from Chanel and Valentino followed, either deconstructing or playing up the prim.

It was at this same time that the blouse found new appreciation, for much the same reason it had the first time around: it became a statement of intent for the pioneering female business executives, some of whom (in the USA at least) wore button-down shirts with loosely tied bows, aping male business attire. 'There were not many women role models so you found guys that you admired how they conducted themselves,' as Hewlett Packard CEO Meg Whitman once noted. 'So we'd wear an interpretation of the man's shirt and tie. I look back at those pictures today and think "what were we thinking?" But it was our attempt to be feminine but fit into what was then a male world.'

In time, the neck area would take a more feminine form with Peter Pan collars, lower top fastenings and the revival of a floppy bow at the neck, a style favoured by Britain's first female prime minister Margaret Thatcher. The origin of the term is uncertain, but a 1934 Anne Adams sewing pattern includes a design for 'an intriguingly feminine pussycat bow tied high under your chin'. One theory has it that, since the pussycat bow was designed to be a softer take on the traditional men's tie, the reference was euphemistically towards female genitalia.

Above: American singer Diana Ross in a tie-front blouse, in 1957.
Below: A model wearing a Dacron and cotton midriff blouse by Gregory during the 1970s.

TWINSET

The simple matching of a trim, often sleeveless, tight-fitting wool sweater with an equally neat, short, round-necked cardigan in the same fabric is first attributed to Austrian designer Otto Weisz, who came up with the pairing for knitwear company Pringle of Scotland in 1934. The 'twin set' was a clever idea, not only commercially – necessitating the purchase of two items of knitwear to achieve the look – but also practically – two layers may well have been in demand at a time of no central heating, especially two that could still give an air of smart formality in the dress of young women striding out into the new world of office work.

The twinset fast won a reputation as the uniform of the secretary, the American college girl and the demure, even when, in the late 1940s and 1950s, Marilyn Monroe and, more suitably given her perceived primness, Grace Kelly were regularly seen wearing the ensemble, albeit in cashmere. The twinset soon became associated with conservatism, with the phrase 'twinset and pearls' a slightly damning term used to describe the habitual look of the well-to-do, schoolmarmish, prim and unfashionable. The style has proved to be a favourite of Queen Elizabeth II throughout her life.

As a style, the twinset has, however, always been in competition with what is perceived, and, in some instances marketed, as its sexier sister, the sweater, its look achieved by a kind of undressing – simply the removal of the cardigan. Worn in a snug fit and with a nipped-in waist to emphasize the breasts, the form-hugging knitwear was favoured by such Hollywood starlets as Jane Russell, Jayne Mansfield, Sophia Loren and Lana Turner. Thanks to her role in the appropriately titled 1937 movie *They Won't Forget* (Mervyn LeRoy), Turner won them the label 'sweater girls', with all that suggested of their particular charms. Underwear manufacturers Berlei, Triumph and Maidenform rushed to provide the right conically shaped 'bullet' bras to underline this 'bombshell' look, while teenage girls in the USA borrowed their mother's twinset cardigan and wore it back to front, buttoned up at the back.

The sweater-girl look was certainly in stark contrast to that of, for example, Audrey Hepburn in *Funny Face* (Stanley Donen, 1957), whose less fitted black polo neck suggested more beatnik chic than brassy sexuality, harking back to Marlene Dietrich's pioneering subversive style of mannish polo neck and trouser suit. Similarly, the key fashion sweater of the 1960s, the ribbed polo neck, pushed by designers Foale & Tuffin and Mary Quant, suggested more a streamlined, unisex, modernistic look than seductive style.

The twinset comes in a variety of lengths and sleeve styles – set-in or raglan, short- or long-sleeved for both the cardigan and the pullover. It is popular among those looking for a retro style, particularly since the huge success of the TV drama series *Mad Men*.

Top: The feel of the twinset proves the difference between Persil washing powder and that of a rival, from an advertisement in 1954. Bottom: Queen Elizabeth II at Windsor Horse Show in 1982.

A woman modelling a Wolsey twinset during
the 1930s.

CROP TOP

Given the historic religious requirement of Indian women's dress to be modest and respectful, that the sometimes scandalously midriff-baring modern-day crop top should have originated centuries ago on the Indian subcontinent makes for an unexpected story. But, the style may well have derived from the choli, the fitted short-sleeve bodice worn under saris. Of course, that is not the only precursor to the crop top: belly dancers of the Middle East also wore the *bedleh*, a heavily beaded version of the style, the beads helping to exaggerate their movement. It is from this that comes the modern romantic notion of crop-topped princesses and genies of the kind to feature in the eighth-century tales of Sinbad the Sailor, which in turn shaped the costume of Barbara Eden in the 1960s hit US sitcom *I Dream of Jeannie* (about a housewife-cum-genie).

It was this show that sparked one of the biggest uptakes of the cropped top as a mainstream fashion item. But it was not the first. Garments that exposed the midriff – daringly so for the times – date to the 1920s as parts of swimming costumes designed by Jean Patou or pioneering cut-outs in dresses by Madeleine Vionnet. It was not until the less conservative 1940s, and the advent of leisurewear as a category of clothing in its own right, however, that cropped tops became more widespread. A burgeoning beach culture and the rise of the beach resort holiday, especially on the West Coast of the USA, saw local firms produce boldly patterned, so-called 'play' clothes that, for example, matched a crop top with tantalizingly short, if high-waisted, shorts. It was the popularity of high-waisted clothing – shorts but more particularly skirts and trousers – that allowed crop tops of all sorts to be worn in both a more chic and more socially acceptable manner. Designers such as Tina Leser and Claire McCardell did much to popularize these styles.

Opposite: American popstar Miley Cyrus exiting the stage door, in New York in 2013.
Below left: A woman in traditional Turkish belly-dancing dress, complete with smoking cigarette, in the 1920s.
Below right: American actress and Olympic swimmer Esther Williams in a cropped lace top in 1945.

The modern concept of the much less reserved crop top – cut high and worn with bottoms cut low – emerged in the 1960s as part of the hippie movement (the midriff perhaps being the female alternative to the male chest, a place on which one could write one's message of love or protest). It was given a fashion spin in the form of 'ethnic' pyjama suits and loose-flowing loungewear also popular at the time, but more strikingly in pieces from John Bates, one of the key designers in 'Swinging London', for whom a crop top was the perfect combination with miniskirts and go-go boots. It was the 1960s that de-eroticized the midriff by exposing it so widely, paving the way for the trend for navel piercing two or more decades on.

Certainly the unforgiving crop top has, since the 1960s, moved in and out of fashion, in no small part down to celebrity seals of approval. In tune with the new interest in aerobics and gym-going in the 1980s, Madonna wore a black mesh crop top in the video for 'Lucky Star' (1983), going on to make the style a staple of her influential lace and leggings aesthetic for the next two years. Britney Spears also revived the look in her video for 'Hit Me Baby One More Time' (1998), while pop star Gwen Stefani also made the crop top her own.

The looser cut-off crop top was very popular throughout the 1980s, while the 1990s saw the introduction of the bustier crop top, a lingerie-styled shirt that revealed the midriff and was often worn under a blazer. Later in the same decade, the T-shirt crop top came to prominence, often depicting graphic logos. Varieties are endless, from the polo-neck version to the cropped tank top and from the short athletic vest to the strapless cropped boob tube.

Below: American pop singer Britney Spears in a cropped T-shirt in 2003.
Opposite: American pop icon Madonna, also in cropped T-shirt and lace for a performance of 'Like a Virgin' in Hollywood in 2003.

T-SHIRT

The blank canvas of the T-shirt has made it an often less-than-subtle means of advertising, be that a company's wares or a political standpoint. When British fashion designer Katharine Hamnett met the then British prime minister Margaret Thatcher in 1984, it was definitely the latter: Hamnett's white, over-sized T-shirt proudly proclaimed in bold black lettering, '58% Don't Want Pershing', a reference to proposed plans to base American nuclear weapons in the UK. Other Hamnett statement T-shirts included 'Education Not Missiles', 'Worldwide Nuclear Ban Now', 'Use a Condom' and the more obscure 'I Love CSP' (concentrated solar power).

T-shirts have been used to promotional ends ever since one was made to announce the release of *The Wizard of Oz* in 1939. They have been widely used as a site for opinions (graphic designer Milton Glaser's much-imitated 'I ❤ NY' of 1977), jokes ('My mum went to Vegas and all I got was this lousy T-shirt'), brand logos (notably after the rise of 'designer' fashion in the 1980s) and campaigns (as in the fashion industry's 'Target' programme to raise awareness of breast cancer). Hamnett might have approved of that, at least. What she did not like was fashion designers 'just printing some inane message,' as she once put it. 'The T-shirt presents the chance to get a message on your chest that can be read 35 feet away and give voice to perhaps taboo subjects.'

This is certainly not in keeping with the origins of the garment, which lie in military attire. The 'T-type' shirt (named after its cut, of course) was devised as underwear for the uniform of US Navy sailors in around 1913 and was originally made from wool. At roughly the same time, the British Army issued its soldiers with a long-sleeved cotton undergarment for service in tropical climates. During World War I, the two allies met in the trenches and a hybrid, short-sleeved cotton garment was created. Although it was sometimes worn by men for sports in the USA during the 1930s ('It's an undershirt. It's an outershirt,' was the slogan used by Sears to sell it in 1938), it was not until images of US servicemen fighting in the Pacific regions were seen back home that it gradually became acceptable to wear the T-shirt as an outer garment in its own right. After the war, ready army surplus supplies and a burgeoning new youth culture made the T-shirt an everyday basic.

This did not mean, however, that the T-shirt lost its rebelliousness: although seen as a garment for men, women embraced the T-shirt during the 1960s thanks both to rock and to wit. During the early 1960s, with the evolution of screen printing and the availability of cheap blank T-shirts, the first band and concert T-shirts emerged. Storm Thorgerson's prism design for Pink Floyd, Stanley Mouse's cover art for the Grateful Dead and John Pasche's 'lick' logo for The Rolling Stones all found themselves emblazoned across chests. The T-shirt, perhaps a little distressed or careworn, became part of the standard look of the rock chick. And, in 1967, graphic designer Warren Dayton was among the first to use the T-shirt in political and pop-art style, devising bold graphics featuring such things as the Statue of Liberty, comic-book excerpts, the *Life* magazine masthead and images of polluted lungs – all T-shirts worn as much by women of the decade's counterculture as by men.

Entrepreneur Don Lick sealed the T-shirt's future as a unisex garment at the end of the 1960s through his quick money-making idea to tie-dye T-shirts, which became symbolic of hippy thinking by the time of the Woodstock Festival in 1969. This opened the door to increasingly bold treatments, not only in sloganeering, but also in colour, cut and texture.

Top: American singer with The Pretenders Chrissie Hynde in a tie-dyed T-shirt in 1986. **Bottom:** A sheer T-shirt, complete with signature caption ('Sanction China'), from designer Katharine Hamnett's Summer 1997 collection.

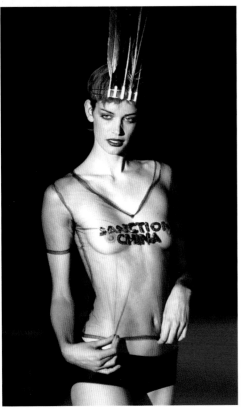

Model Bebe Buell poses for a portrait wearing
a *Creem* magazine T-shirt in 1980.

TUBE TOP

The tube top has its origin in a production mistake in a clothing factory, which resulted in a job lot of fabric tubes in an Indian-print elastic gauze. Some of these found their way to 50 West 17th Street and Murray Kleid's S&M Fringing, New York's largest women's accessories store. There they stayed, mostly ignored, until Elie Tahari, Israeli fashion designer and new immigrant to the USA, spotted them – and their potential – at the start of the 1970s. He bought them for $2 and sold them for twice as much. Soon after, he was taking orders for thousands, and he began manufacturing them in 1973, eventually building a $500-million-a-year business.

'It was an East Village happening: "I am not wearing a bra! I am a modern hippie girl!",' is how Tahari explained the tube top's appeal, adding the tube top was 'totally disco'. When covered with sequins and worn with heels and skintight jeans, the tube top was the perfect garment for the crowd at legendary New York nightclub Studio 54, practising their *Saturday Night Fever* moves.

By the 1980s, the tube top was mainstream enough to be considered sufficiently respectable office attire, albeit under a tailored jacket. But, it was the film about the disco period – *The Last Days of Disco* (Whit Stillman, 1998) – that induced a major fashion revival for the sparkly style in the late 1990s and early 2000s, one which was quickly picked up on by popstar Britney Spears, who in turn influenced teen fashion, and the Carrie Bradshaw character in the fashion-focused US series *Sex and the City*. Come 2012, the tube top was back again in new, dressier form, thanks to Prada and Versace.

The tube top may have had an unelasticated precursor back in the early 1950s, which *Vogue* editor Diana Vreeland championed as beachwear, but, in fact, a similar style can be traced back much further to fourth-century Greece, where women wore it to swim in. Thanks to fabrics woven with elastic, the incarnation in the 1970s was a new idea: simple and comfortable but tight, clingy and revealing. By being strapless, it was sometimes too revealing: a few years after its launch, the tube top won a kind of infamy thanks to the USA game show *The Price is Right*, in which contestants were selected at random from the audience. When her name was called out during the recording, in 1979, one audience member jumped up in excitement, and her tube top came down. 'She came on down,' host Bob Barker told the audience [a reference to the show's 'Come on down!' catchphrase], 'and they came on out'. Small wonder, perhaps, that in the UK the tube top was better known as the boob tube.

The tube top went on to provide the basis for many other garments, from tube-top smocks to tube-top dresses and, applying the same idea further down the body, tube skirts. Their development was assisted by an ever-more-sophisticated variety of fabrics – spandex, stretch nylon, Lycra – that allowed the garment to cling, to stay up securely (some makers even applied an adhesive band on the inside to make sure) and to hold its shape.

Top: A model on the Paris catwalk for Maison IRFE's S/S 2014 show.
Left: American actress Sarah-Jessica Parker wears a tube top for a scene for US hit TV series *Sex and the City*.
Opposite: Promotional portrait of American singer and actress Cher for *The Sonny and Cher Comedy Hour*, 1972.

6.
UNDERWEAR

tights / bra / slip / corset

TIGHTS

Stockings may have the sensual advantage, but it is in the more humble pair of tights that comfort and practicality are found. Perhaps it is no coincidence that pantyhose, as they are known in the USA, became popular in the 1960s, an era of women's liberation and of more revealing fashion. Indeed, by the time Mary Quant had pioneered the miniskirt in the 1960s, she was already selling branded tights. Tights even managed to attain some sex appeal during this period, in no small part down to Brigitte Bardot, who was photographed otherwise naked in a pair.

The now commonplace item – machine-knitted from often advanced textiles into a one-piece garment – was not how the design started out. Originals were called pantyhose for their simple combination of 'panties' and 'hose', comprising underwear and stockings sewn together as one, with the intention of covering the legs without breezy gaps while also minimizing the need for extra undergarments.

Quite who can claim to have invented the style remains debatable, although, ironically perhaps given their stereotypical love of stockings, it was a man. Allen Grant, of the Californian company Glen Raven Knitting Mills, devised what he called 'Panti-Legs' in 1953, although it took another six years to bring them to market. Meanwhile, in 1956, Ernest Rice filed for patent on his design for 'combination stockings and panty', the design of which became industry standard. Pantyhose were not an instant success: knitting the flat pieces together and creating the rear seam associated with stockings of the period were time-consuming and expensive procedures, at least until the invention of the circular knitting machine, which allowed cheaper, seam-free styles to enter the market in 1958. Their popularity was increased by their necessity after the introduction of the miniskirt.

The garment did retain some allure, at least in linguistic terms; in the USA, pantyhose continued to refer to items of a low denier near transparency. This made them more akin to 'peelable' stockings, which were hugely popular through the 1940s and 1950s thanks to the invention by DuPont chemist Wallace Carothers of nylon, patented in 1935 and introduced to the world in 1938. Nylon made pantyhose accessible, cheaper and, perhaps most appealingly, form-fitting, unlike their silk predecessors. The term 'tights', in contrast to 'pantyhose', was used to refer to thicker, opaque and often woollen styles worn in winter.

This description of tights was, in fact, closer to stockings or hose, as they were originally conceived in the sixteenth century, when they were made from coloured wool or silk, and worn under breeches by men only (European society did not permit women's clothing to reveal any part of the leg, an idea that would last until the early twentieth century). A 'good leg' was a supposed indication of male virility: 'Remember who commended thy yellow stockings ... And wished to see thee cross-gartered,' as Malvolio says in Shakespeare's *Twelfth Night*.

The term 'cross-gartered' referred to the fashion for decorating hose with overlapping ribbons, and was an insight into the future of tights 400 years later. It was not until the 1970s that tights, until this moment plain, dark and ubiquitous, were considered a site for self-expression thanks to advances in textile technology and the invention of Lycra and spandex. The decade saw the introduction of coloured and patterned versions, with Dior, for example, famously offering 101 alternatives.

Below: A poster for the movie *Rolled Stockings* of 1927.
Opposite: Blondie front-woman Debbie Harry rocks in coloured tights, 1979.

"ROLLED STOCKINGS"

JAMES HALL · LOUISE BROOKS · RICHARD ARLEN
NANCY PHILLIPS AND EL BRENDEL
Directed by RICHARD ROSSON
Story by FREDERICA SAGOR
Screen play by PERCY HEATH

BRA

That the history of the bra incorporates a series of experiments in engineering is perhaps best illustrated by the part played by Howard Hughes, the oil magnate, eccentric innovator and film-maker who believed that Jane Russell's already impressive cleavage was not quite impressive enough. This was in 1941, during the filming of *The Outlaw*, and Hughes set to work using his knowledge of aviation design to create the first cantilevered bra, with steel rods connected to the straps, resulting in a shelf-like bust. The contraption was, however, so uncomfortable that during filming Russell is said to have worn her own bra padded with tissues. The result was much the same, and the Hollywood Production Code Administration ordered 30 seconds of film of Russell's bosom to be removed before it passed the film.

That, at least, is how the story goes, although it could be an urban myth or a publicity stunt devised by Hughes. But it still points to the bra as the place where physics meets fashion, as seen later in *Desperately Seeking Susan* (Susan Seidelman, 1985), which introduced the idea of underwear as outerwear, one later developed by Jean-Paul Gaultier for Madonna's 'Blonde Ambition' tour in 1990. It also highlights the lengths to which underwear designers go to give not only comfort and support, but also added lift, separation and cleavage. Feminists have argued that these traits objectify women, expressing this most poignantly by throwing bras, washing-up liquid and false eyelashes, among other items, into what they termed the 'Freedom Trash Can' at the 1968 Miss America competition in Atlantic City.

The history of the bra, however, goes back much further, to 1866, when the first styles, produced from wire and silk and making no concession to comfort, appeared in the UK and later in the USA. In 1889, a French corset-maker, Herminie Cadolle, developed her *bien-être* or 'well-being', a corset–bra hybrid in which the breasts were

Opposite: Italian actress Gina Lollobrigida in 1973.
Below left: A poster for the Howard Hughes western *The Outlaw* (1943), featuring a buttressed Jayne Mansfield.
Below right: Marpessa Hennink wearing Italian lingerie by Ferdinando Scianna in 1989.

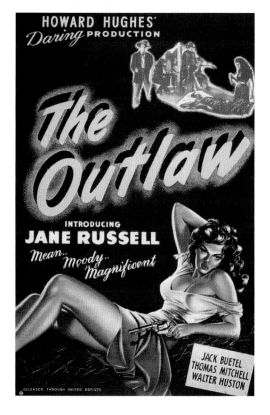

supported by cups and shoulder straps. Four years later, Marie Tucek patented her 'breast supporter'. With its shoulder straps and hook-and-eye closure, it was arguably the first recognizably modern bra. It was also an idea Cadolle worked with; in 1905, she separated her hybrid design into a waist corset and a bra, calling the latter a *soutien-gorge* or 'chest support', as the bra is still known in France.

By the 1920s and aided by the decline of corset-wearing during World War I due to women taking up factory work and the need to ration materials, bra design had moved on again. Between 1922 and 1928, Ida and William Rosenthal, founders of Maidenform, together with Enid Bissett, laid claim to creating the first bra with distinct cups and the notion of sizing the cups (though it would not be until 1935 that the underwear manufacturer Warner would introduce the now standard A to D – and beyond – cup-size system).

The evolution of the bra did not stop there, as designs to provide comfort segued into those to offer artificial enhancement of the bust. In 1947, Frederick Mellinger, founder of Frederick's of Hollywood – and, one might note, a man, as he said, shamelessly making garments ultimately for male pleasure – created the first padded bra. A year later, he devised the first push-up bra, sold under the fantastic name of 'The Rising Star'. More amusing still, his cone-shaped bras were called 'Missiles'.

These were not, however, expressions of a new idea. The development of the cone-shaped bra during the 1930s was deliberately intended to accentuate the bust; those women who wore them were nicknamed 'sweater girls' (see p.112), after the original sweater girl, actress Lana Turner, who introduced the look in *They Won't Forget* (Mervyn LeRoy, 1937). Indeed, the first bra-like prototype on record was similarly concerned with aesthetics over support; dating to 1859, it was designed by an American called Henry Lesher and incorporated inflatable pads. Again following fashion, the first 'Backless Brassiere', patented by New York socialite Mary Phelps Jacob in 1914, was designed not to enhance the bust but to flatten it.

Decade by decade, the appeal of the enhanced bust would rise and fall, but, perhaps inevitably, it would mostly rise. The boyish look gave way to the ultra-curvy, with Canadian designer Louise Poirier creating the Wonderbra in 1964 – a wonder of textile construction, comprising some 54 parts, and, in future years, a wonder of billboard advertising, thanks to its 'Hello, Boys' campaign of 1994, featuring a bra-clad Eva Herzigova looking down appreciatively at her cleavage. She was not the only one; several traffic accidents were attributed to it, too.

Below: Madonna performing in Jean-Paul Gaultier-designed bra top during her 'Blonde Ambition' tour of 1990.
Opposite: A model poses in a strapless inflatable brassiere, designed for wearing under evening dresses, 1952.

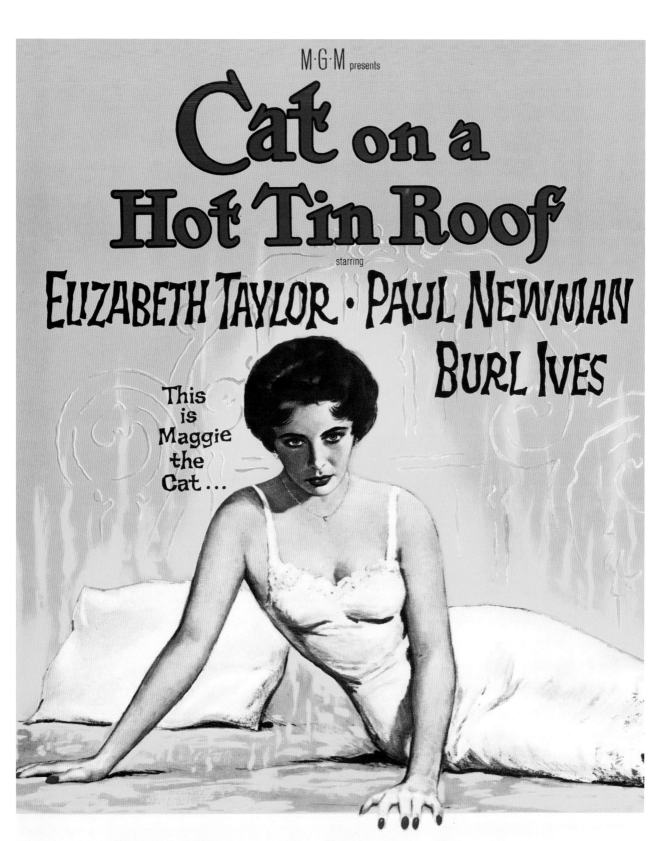

SLIP

Some might believe that the bra was the first instance of underwear becoming outerwear, during the 1980 and '90s, or perhaps the camisole's gradual transition from lingerie to top. But, it had happened before. The slip, devised in the 1920s as a silken undergarment, was essentially an extended camisole that allowed the more close-fitting, boyish clothes of the era to be worn, while smoothing one's outward appearance in the process. However, the period was also one of growing emancipation for women and, consequently, the corseted restrictions of Edwardian fashion were being rejected. The slip – svelte, tactile, gently loose and, with those spaghetti straps, very comfortable – proposed itself as an ideal outer garment. The archetypal, straight-lined, sleek dress favoured by the flappers was, in effect, a slip in more substantial, modesty-saving fabric.

It was an insufficiently liberated time for women to wear an actual slip as a dress, even if the following decade saw slips becoming more sophisticated still. Cut on the bias, after the idea was introduced by Madeleine Vionnet in 1927, they sat more closely to the figure, like a second skin, and had subtle embellishment around the bust. But the world had changed by 1949. One story has it that a New York fashion model called Anna-Lee Danels and Henry Callahan, designer and window-display artist for lingerie company Lord & Taylor, decided to demonstrate that the slips of the time were so minimalistic, and often luxurious, that they could pass for dresses proper. So they went out to all the best places – the famed Stork Club, a masked ball at the Waldorf Astoria, the El Morocco lounge – to test the theory, with a photographer from a magazine in tow. Danels's slip passed without comment, despite its obviously provocative, sexy suggestion of underwear, nightwear and négligées.

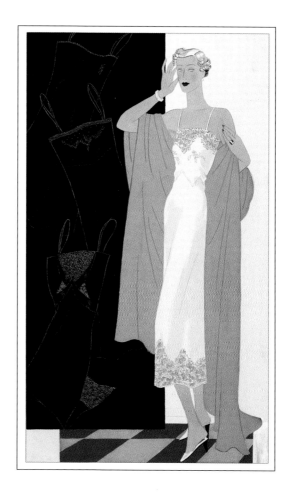

Opposite: A poster for *Cat on a Hot Tin Roof* **(1958) starring Elizabeth Taylor as Maggie – in her, for the time, provocatively revealing slip. Right: A fashion illustration from the 1930s featuring a model in a silk crêpe slip.**

It would be almost another ten years before relaxed regulations – most notably in the USA – finally allowed women to appear in their underwear in advertising imagery, in the movies and in magazines, a moment that made the slip the star of the new boudoir dressing. Elizabeth Taylor's appearance in a white slip in the 1958 movie *Cat On a Hot Tin Roof* (Richard Brooks) further spread its innocent-cum-sassy appeal – even if Taylor's was fully lined by its designer Helen Rose to ensure no transparency would upset watchful censors.

The slip went through a resurgence of popularity in the 1990s, in no small part down to British designer John Galliano, who further refined the bias-cut version, 'a symbol of what women wore at night,' as *Vogue* editor Anna Wintour called it. This time there was no concern about hiding what lay beneath. Models, increasingly regarded as benchmarks of style, were said to favour them because they were easy to take on and off when changing for shoots. But when waif-like Kate Moss wore a see-through silver version by Liza Bruce to her model agency's 'Look of the Year' party in 1993, attention certainly increased. That decade, the slip even shed its obvious femininity, when it was worn over a white T-shirt, with baggy sweater and chunky footwear, in the grunge style of Hole frontwoman Courtney Love. Love did also wear it in more glamorous style on occasion, however.

Left: American rock singer Courtney Love, with her daughter, arriving at a Los Angeles awards ceremony in 1992.
Opposite: British model Kate Moss wears a transparent slip dress to an industry part in London in 1993.

CORSET

As influential on fashion trends as Madonna has been, when she performed for her 'Blond Ambition' tour in 1990 she sparked demand for a most unexpected garment: the corset. She wore one in dusky pink, with conical cups, a creation of French designer Jean-Paul Gaultier, who was responsible for introducing the idea of underwear as outerwear in his 1983 'Dada' collection. He had based it on a design he had first made in paper for his teddy bear as a child. 'It was slightly sadomasochistic for a teddy bear really, and the first transgender teddy-bear at that,' Gaultier noted, 'but it was held together with lots of safety pins, so was quite punk as well.'

Gaultier went on to design corsets for Kylie Minogue, too. And, with the rise of influential new lingerie companies such as Joe Corré's Agent Provocateur in 1994, and the revival of burlesque performance towards the end of the decade, the corset underwent a revival that might have astounded many women less than a generation before.

In the mid-1970s, Vivienne Westwood was the first designer of the twentieth century to use the corset in its original form since Poiret had rejected it at the start of the century. Although corset dresses by such designers as Dolce & Gabbana and Thierry Mugler came into style during the 1980s, the corset element was actually a softer construction that suggested its supposed sexiness without the restrictions. The corset proper had been for the best part of a century a symbol of the oppression of women. It was worn to meet society's expectations – yes, of fashion, but also of the ideal, hourglass feminine form.

World War I and the boyish flapper fashion that followed signalled the slow demise of any form of corsetry. But not before it had enjoyed centuries at the heart of women's attire. The corset had, in variously restrictive forms, been worn since the early-to-mid sixteenth century, notably by those well-to-do women who could afford the often complex constructions of lacing and, later, horn or whalebone stiffeners that eroticized by exaggerating curves, lifting up and unifying the bosom and squeezing in the waist, but which also literally rearranged one's internal organs and threatened one's ability to breath.

Tellingly, the metal eyelet, now commonly found on shoes, was invented in 1828 to allow the corset to endure greater stress while being laced; while 1900 saw the introduction in Paris of a new S-shaped style that held the torso straight but, as fashion dictated, pushed the hips back. It was said to alleviate pressure on the ribs and so was marketed as the 'health corset'.

Women had last worn some form of girdle-like, shape-enforcing foundation garment in the 1960s, before a revolution in fabric technology, in fashion and in gender politics made it look antiquated. Now, here the corset was again, 40 years on, this time more knowingly bawdy, and typically in comfortable stretch fabrics – a symbol of empowerment, perhaps, or maybe just of sexual objectification. Indeed, liberated from being hidden as an undergarment, the new corset obviously nodded to fetishwear and lingerie's sexy stereotype of bustier, stockings and suspenders.

Top: A colour-tinted plate of cabaret artist Margill, in corset bodice, in c. 1900.
Left: Pop singer Madonna in the Jean-Paul Gaultier-designed cone-bra corset, during her 'Blonde Ambition' tour of 1990.
Opposite: A dress comprising corset-like bodice and gathered skirt by Gianni Versace from the S/S 1995 collection.

MG86990

7.

LEISURE AND SWIMWEAR

swimming costume / bikini / jumpsuit / leotard

SWIMMING COSTUME

In an age of biomimetic technologies, tan-through fabrics and a skimpiness that makes the swimming costume a bikini in all but name, it is hard to imagine that in the Victorian era, when the development of the railways first allowed ready transport to the coast, and the idea of the seaside holiday and public bathing first developed, women would don bathing dresses made of serge or dark flannel. Their name – bathing dresses – indicates the moral agenda of the day: that women should remain as covered up as possible, regardless of the activity at hand. Even today, the use of the word 'costume' suggests that this is clothing worn for an event regarded as being somehow outside the social norm.

The only concessions to practicality were that on occasion the jacket had short sleeves and that, beneath a knee-length skirt, a pair of trousers was worn. This was the first time that women wearing trousers was tolerated, although wearing trousers as daywear would not tentatively enter fashion until the 1920s. Changes to swimwear were slow, revealing a touch more flesh with each evolution: cap sleeves exposed the upper arm, for example, and then shorter bloomers a flash of calf.

It was not until the twentieth century that anything like a made-for-purpose garment came into fashion, and even then the figure-hugging, sleeveless 'tank suits' of the 1920s, inspired by Portland Knitting Company's 1913 swimsuit design for men, were still made of wool and still had propriety front of mind. A switch to printed cottons and a backless, shorter cut – sometimes inspired by the new fashion for sunbathing, but just as often worn with a mid-thigh-length overskirt dubbed the 'modesty apron' – was introduced in the 1930s, when the all-in-one swimming costume finally became a subject of style.

Opposite: Marilyn Monroe deep into James Joyce's *Ulysses* and in a stripy swimsuit, in 1955.
Below: Painter Arthur C. Michael's design for a poster showing fashionable beach dress of the 1930s, produced for Southern Railway and London and North Eastern Railway.

THE BELGIAN COAST
VIA HARWICH-ZEEBRUGGE OR DOVER-OSTEND
Information from Continental Departments, L·N·E·R Liverpool Street Station, London, E.C.2., or Southern Railway, Victoria Station, London, S.W.I. or principal L·N·E·R and S.R. Offices and Agencies

Hollywood helped to dictate trends in no small part due to a new interest in synchronized swimming or 'water ballet', a sport that developed in the USA over the next 10 years and was reflected in a spate of 'aqua musicals' that made stars of Dorothy Lamour and, more notably, Esther Williams, whose first Technicolor film, *Bathing Beauty* (George Sidney, 1944), popularized the term. Companies such as Cole of California – which did much to prettify swimsuits with sequins, beads and prints – created 'The Esther Williams' swimsuit ('Like Esther, this swimsuit has everything,' read one advert), and Williams eventually launched her own swimwear line. A readiness for starlets to be snapped poolside helped to spread the more glamorous trends and to increase the profile of Rita Hayworth and Betty Grable (the highest paid Hollywood celebrity of the period, whose famed and oft-exposed legs were insured for $1million).

As self-consciousness grew in the 1940s, no doubt prompted by the fashion for close-fitting, high, straight-cut swimsuits, underwear manufacturers entered the market to offer swimwear stretch 'control panels' – many using Lastex, a latex-based elastic thread developed by Dunlop in the 1930s – and bust support, allowing the first strapless styles to be created. It was the widespread use of Lastex's replacement, Lycra, and of nylon in the 1960s that brought about a more revealing and distinctive style of swimsuit, in part because it was now in competition with the more commonplace bikini. Cut-out sections, perhaps filled in with mesh or plastic rings, and a higher-cut leg were among the developments that, textile science aside, brought the swimming costume into the modern era, with only increased exposure to come.

And, sometimes in a big way. In 1964, designer, provocateur and nudist Rudi Gernreich introduced the monokini, a topless swimsuit. While it inspired a fad for topless nightclubbing, it did not initially catch on as beachwear; Gernreich actually intended it as a protest against a repressive society rather than as a commercial product. 'Women drop their bikini tops already, so it seemed like the natural next step,' Gernreich said at the time. By the 1980s, however, it did achieve a brief popularity – albeit in opposition to a concurrent trend for more athletic, racer-style swimsuits that echoed the looks of the 1920s. Gernreich's subsequent attempt to launch a 'pubikini' – exposing the pubic area – did not, unsurprisingly, achieve any popularity at all.

Top: American actress Ann Miller in c. 1950.
Bottom: The definitive pin-up of World War II, American actress Betty Grable – her legs were insured by her studio for $1million.
Opposite: A colour-tinted sepia plate of a fashionable swimsuit style for 1910.

BIKINI

When Ursula Andress emerges from the sea in the first James Bond movie *Dr. No* (Terence Young, 1962), it is not her collection of shells or diving knife that impresses. What made the moment a classic of cinematic sexiness is Andress's bikini, designed for the scene by costumier Tessa Prendergast. It signalled a key transition in womenswear, too: the one-piece swimsuit (see p.139), itself only respectable since the turn of the twentieth century, before which time women were expected to bathe in an ankle-length garment, was out. The bikini – all curves and strategic erotic revelation – was in for good. In the same year, it was on the cover of *Playboy*, and, in 1964, on the cover of the inaugural swimsuit issue of *Sports Illustrated*.

The sexual revolution of the 1960s may have diminished the bikini's power to shock, yet this was a testament to the speed of social evolution. Just 16 years previously, in July 1946, the inventor of the bikini struggled to find a model who would wear it. Its radicalism was tantamount to outright indecency. Louis Réard, a one-time car engineer, had to turn to a nude dancer, Micheline Bernardini, to wear the skimpy style at its unveiling at the trendy Piscine Molitor swimming pool in the centre of Paris. The effect was as predicted: an international media storm, an immediate ban in the Catholic countries of Italy, Spain and Portugal, as well as in Australia and Belgium, and general disregard in the USA. 'It is inconceivable that any girl with tact and decency would even wear such a thing,' opined *Modern Girl* magazine in 1957.

Not for nothing had Réard named his beach style after Bikini Atoll in the South Pacific where the first nuclear weapons were tested by the US military in the same year. He expected it to be just as explosive. And, no wonder: even the original bikini was small, requiring just 76cm (30 inches) of fabric. It 'wasn't a bikini unless it could be pulled through a wedding ring,' claimed his advertisement for the new style.

All this did not dissuade the French. Some 50,000 people wrote fan letters to Réard and a race for ever tinier bikinis seemed to begin. Also in 1946, Parisian designer Jacques Heim introduced the 'Atome'. With a nod towards the weapon of mass destruction, the name also hinted at its size: this, it claimed, was the world's smallest swimsuit yet, more a weapon of mass distraction.

The definitive moment for swimwear in cinema: Ursula Andress emerging from the sea in *Dr. No* (1962).

Over the next decade, the French Riviera rapidly made the bikini its own, with movie starlets such as Brigitte Bardot at the Cannes Film Festival, finding it a perfect magnet for the paparazzi. So much so, that, in the USA, Marilyn Monroe, Jayne Mansfield and the 'Million Dollar Mermaid' Esther Williams soon followed her lead. In 1960, Brian Hyland said it all with his hit 'Itsy Bitsy Teenie Weenie Yellow Polka Dot Bikini', as the style entered pop culture. From Annette Funicello in *Beach Party* (William Asher, 1963), one of a new wave of surfing movies, to the pre-historic interpretation offered by Raquel Welch in *One Million Years B.C.* (Don Chaffey, 1966), the bikini was everywhere.

For all the fuss, the idea of a two-piece swimsuit was not a new one, albeit that taking it to such minimalism was. Two-piece garments were worn for exercising by ancient Romans and Greeks. Carl Jantzen designed a two-piece style, akin to swim-shorts and a thigh-length vest, back in 1913. Even this was enough to cause some scandal: six years earlier, Australian swimmer Annette Kellerman had been arrested in Boston, Massachusetts, for wearing a figure-hugging one-piece. But it was not enough to stop the style taking hold. From then on, there was a gradual creep towards increasing amounts of exposed flesh, with even wartime fabric rationing playing its role in shortening and cropping the swimsuit's constituent parts. It would take another 40 years but, thanks in part to a fashion for tanning, the bikini would eventually reach a point of maximum exposure just short of nudity with the tanga, thong and Brazilian G-string.

Above: American actress Betty Grable in a yellow two-piece swimsuit in the 1940s.
Right: A young Brigitte Bardot posing on the beach during the Cannes Film Festival of 1953.

JUMPSUIT

An ideal example of a garment that is utterly utilitarian in its origins, yet, thanks to tweaks of cut and choice of fabric, able to achieve the kind of glamour typically reserved for an evening dress. The jumpsuit is, after all, anti-fashion in more ways than one. It took its cue from the protective overalls of factory workers, aviators, firefighters, racing drivers and skiers and from a siren-suit-style garment that could be put on in a hurry, as fan Winston Churchill recognized. Yet it also represented the kind of outfit worn in the future when society had found fashion redundant, a future that could be technological and shiny or dark and dystopian. The workers of George Orwell's *1984* would wear a jumpsuit.

Certainly, it was among the Futurists of the early twentieth century that the jumpsuit found its first expression beyond the world of manual labour. In 1919, the Florentine painter Ernesto Michahelles (Thayaht) proposed a minimalistic version in cotton and canvas – cut in a T-shape and fastened with buttons and a belt – to subvert fashion's pretensions and as a means of freeing its wearer from the constraints of having to consider one's dress on a daily basis. As unisex as the garment was, it seemed all the more subversive on a woman, even though many women had worked on factory floors across Europe during World War I, which had ended the previous year. In 1923, the Russian constructivist Aleksandr Rodchenko and his wife Vavara Stepanova began wearing 'production clothing', a single-piece overall made by Stepanova. It revived the idea of the jumpsuit as the most practical, uncomplicated and logical of everyday garments.

Elsa Schiaparelli was the first bona fide fashion designer to dabble with the idea of bringing the jumpsuit out of the world of functionality and into the world of fashion in the 1930s. Her garment was part practical, part stylish, coming in light blue with a hood, braided cuffs,

Opposite: American actress Heather Locklear poses for a fashion shoot in 1981.
Below: American actress Lana Turner getting comfortable in a sleeveless v-neck jumpsuit in 1955.

ankles and waist and even a water bottle to be worn across the body. Up until the end of the 1950s, jumpsuits were worn by women on the construction line for the war effort – leading to Norman Rockwell's iconic 'Rosie the Riveter' propaganda image in *The Saturday Evening Post* – while more show-stopping versions were sported by Hollywood stars Katharine Hepburn (in a monogramed silk number), Veronica Lake and Lauren Bacall.

Perhaps unsurprisingly, it was an ex-bomber pilot, Emilio Pucci, who in 1960 first fully introduced the idea of the jumpsuit as a catwalk fashion item, produced in his patented fabric Emilioform, a synthetic jersey. He was quickly followed by society designer Irene Galitzine, who produced palazzo pants with a bib-style top to create a more feminine jumpsuit, and Norma Kamali, while space-age versions appeared by André Courrèges and Pierre Cardin. In the UK, however, Diana Rigg – playing Emma Peel in a skintight leather number by costume designer John Bates for television series *The Avengers* – really drove the style home. Valentino showed a jumpsuit, too, first in 1966 and again in 1971, when he dispelled any connotations of manual labour by making it white, with the top tailored like a double-breasted jacket. It was a long way from the 2012 'onesie' romper-suit fad.

By the 1970s, the jumpsuit in all permutations – backless, flared, knitted, stretch, with outsize collars or halter-neck – had become a fashion staple. The style was a favourite of all four members of Abba, and was regularly seen at New York's landmark nightclub Studio 54. In silver and synthetic materials, it also gained a glam-rock edge, although Suzi Quatro would only ever wear one made from black leather. Since then, Dolce & Gabbana created a tuxedo jumpsuit for Madonna and Prada produced a version in plaid silk, while Givenchy offered a multi-pocketed design. Designers as diverse as Stella McCartney, Thierry Mugler, Yohji Yamamoto and Yves Saint Laurent have all kept the style at the forefront of fashion.

Opposite: A model wearing a striped 'laundry bag' jumpsuit from designer Geoffrey Beene's 'Beene Bag' collection of 1975.
Below: Norman Rockwell's illustration of 'Rosie The Riveter', for the cover of *The Saturday Evening Post* **in 1943.**

LEOTARD

Increased interest in health and fitness during the 1980s saw exercise reconsidered as an activity for all, and beyond the traditional realms of school gym and sports field. The exercise class rapidly became the accessible means of enjoying a routine of organized high-energy movement under expert tuition. Aerobics became the lifestyle buzzword, and particular clothes were required: sweatbands, leg warmers, cropped cardigans (the latter two items being borrowed from ballet attire) and, most memorably, the leotard.

But, it was not just the term aerobics that was old by this point – it was coined in 1968 – so was the leotard. The tight-fitting garment, originally with full-length sleeves and legs, and entered by the neck, was first worn by the man who gave it its name, Jules Léotard, in 1859. Léotard was a flying-trapeze artist and, although his special attire was made in knitted jersey – rather than such stretch fabrics as DuPont's Lycra spandex with which it would much later be associated – the story has it that this was sufficiently revealing of his male physique to be a draw in itself.

Although the idea of such a snug garment was not new in Léotard's time – versions had been worn under more diaphanous styles of clothing since the late eighteenth century – it was his that caught on. It sparked a trend and was worn by a wide variety of artistes, especially those involved in the performing arts of circus, burlesque and ballet. Legend has it that male ballet dancers wore a full-length body suit under fitted trunks until, in the early twentieth century, pioneering Russian dancer Vaslav Nijinsky forgot to don the shorts for a dance.

The revealing nature of the leotard, covering up and yet seemingly showing all, was only enhanced when activewear company Danskin first made it in spandex. Its designer, Bonnie August, had 'got almost everybody going around in next to nothing', as *People* magazine suggested in 1979. August saw the potential for the leotard to be worn as much as a fashion item, with a short skirt, for example, as a sports garment, although the Californian roller skaters of the era saw the leotard as fit for both purposes. A colour palette of garish brights and neon detailing was favoured, yellow, purple and electric blue were especially popular, and Lycra was made a household name.

Above: Madonna well dressed for a high-energy dance routine for 'Confessions on a Dance Floor' (2006).
Right: American actress Jamie Lee Curtis in *Perfect* (1985), a drama set around the decade's health-club craze.

With the popularity of the video-cassette recorder – first made commercial in 1964 but not widespread in homes until the Betamax/VHS format wars of the early 1980s – aerobics exercise at home also took off. The likes of the million-selling *Jane Fonda's Workout* (1982) – just one of the movie star's 23 exercise videos – ensured aerobics style went global. By then, popular culture could only underline the fashionability of the leotard, although, with the love of leotards among more extravagant performers of rock and pop from Van Halen's David Lee Roth to Queen's Freddie Mercury, men were introduced to the style. The video for Olivia Newton-John's song 'Physical' (1981), the television series *Fame* (1982), movies *Flashdance* (Adrian Lyne, 1983), *Heavenly Bodies* (Peter Jackson, 1984) and *Perfect* (James Bridges, 1985) with John Travolta and Jamie Lee Curtis, all made the leotard the look of the moment on the street as much as in the dance studio.

At least for a while. More relaxed, more forgiving clothing took over for sports and exercise. But the leotard was adopted by such designers as Donna Karan in 1985 and repurposed as a means of covering up under semi-transparent clothing, and as a super-smooth alternative to a blouse under a tailored jacket. It was precisely because the leotard was so closely associated with the late 1970s and early 1980s that it could have such a retro fashion impact years later, when Madonna prompted a brief revival after wearing one designed by Jean-Paul Gaultier for her 2006 tour.

Below left: 'Bernarr MacFadden Reveals the Secret of "High Powered Health", on the cover of *Physical Culture* magazine, 1926.
Below right: The Yugoslavia-born actress Sylvia Koscina exercises and preens in Rome, 1964.

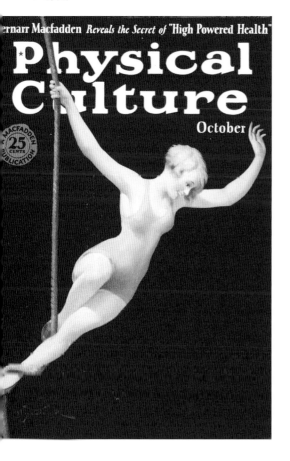

8.

SHOES

stiletto / platform / ballet pump / riding boot / sandal / plimsoll / cowboy boot / kitten heel / peep-toe & slingback / wedge

Manolo Blahnik stilettos and Roger Vivier
clutch, photographed by Patrick Demarchelier
in 'Red is the New Black' photo shoot for
Vogue, 2004.

STILETTO

No style of shoe has been as much the subject of desirability, status, fetish and controversy as the stiletto. In its most towering and most reduced form, the stiletto was designed by Roger Vivier for Dior in 1954, with the intention that its narrow toe, low-cut vamp and *talon aiguille* (needle heel), a thin, tapered, 8cm (5 inches) heel (like the stiletto dagger), would suggest one thing: sex. And, sex as a blunt counter to the grey deprivations of the post-war 1940s, at that.

As shoe designer Manolo Blahnik noted: 'The thing is that wearing shoes like these transforms you, the way you feel, the way your buttocks move. That's what's sexy, not the shoes.' This idea was not lost on many screen sirens of the 1940s onwards, not least Marilyn Monroe, who famously had her shoes made with one heel slightly shorter than the other, to emphasize the sway of her hips.

An advance in engineering during those grey 1940s had made such a particularly high heel feasible. Metal extrusion had allowed for the production of short lengths of thin but extremely strong steel rods, which André Perugia may well have used to produce a stiletto-type shoe ahead of Vivier. But the idea of the heel itself was not new. High heels in some form were worn by ancient civilizations: in Egypt, by butchers to keep them above the piles of offal; in Rome as an indicator that the wearer was a prostitute; and in China, where concubines wore them to express their sexual availability, although it is believed that Venetian women of the sixteenth century first wore them for reasons of style.

Then, as now, they provoked debate: one claim was that the style was invented by husbands to make their wives' movement awkward and love affairs consequently less likely. They were much more difficult to walk in then as, until the 1800s, the shoes were produced (ill-fittingly)

Sketches of designs from the shoe designer who popularized stilettos through the 1980s, Manolo Blahnik.

to be worn on either foot, so technically hard was it to make high heels to accommodate left and right feet. If the high heel had a champion, it was Catherine de Medici (1519–89), future wife of Henry II of France, and as such a huge influence in matters of fashion. Her conflation of height with stature in society (hence the phrase 'well-heeled) saw her take to wearing 5cm-high heels (2 inches), a move also emulated by Mary Tudor.

Two centuries on, and the outward elegance of European court life was expressed by ever more streamlined and refined styles of heel, along with the first inklings that they could provide a new form of eroticism. This led the Puritans in America's fledgling colonies to legislate against the wearing of the style to entrap a man. Furthermore, after the French Revolution (1789–99), Napoleon banned them in the spirit of equality, both between classes and between men and women.

It would not be until the mid-nineteenth century that the high heel would make a return, and with a vengeance. At sometimes 15cm (6 inches), the heel exaggerated a pronounced in-step, thought to be an expression of good breeding. The high heel was even said to help backache rather than cause it. While the fetishization of the high heel continued apace, by the twentieth century the style's popularity was subject largely to the vagaries of fashion, aside, that is, from claims by women's rights supporters that the style represented a repressive, contemporary form of foot binding, rather than a source of pleasure or power for women.

With the late twentieth century seeing shoe design reappraised as a skill in its own right – rather than secondary to fashion design – stilettos have won a new cachet and collectability, notably those by Blahnik ('slut pumps', as the comedian Joan Rivers dubbed them) and Christian Louboutin, whose signature ruby red soles (see p. 178) echoed the red heels (or *les talons rouges*) which only aristocracy could wear in Louis XIV's France.

Below: An advertisement shot by Guy Bourdin for the Charles Jourdan A/W collection, 1977. **Opposite:** Lady Gaga talks with *The Morning Mash Up Live* in New York City, 2013.

PLATFORM

Since the early twentieth century, the platform has often been considered something of a curiosity. In 1939, an advert for the Beachcraft Sandal Company of New York, for example, proclaimed its new platform design to be a 'novel idea in wooden soles'. The same year, a cartoon in the *Boot and Shoe Recorder*, an American trade publication, saw a shoe salesman telling a woman trying on a pair of platforms that 'they'll make you tower over your husband Mrs. Green!'

At the time, it would have been considered unusual to wear a platform shoe on the street; in the USA, the style had first found popularity in 1938 specifically as beachwear, a development on the layered cork platform shoes designed by the likes of Salvatore Ferragamo for similar purposes on the French Riviera and Mediterranean coastal resorts the year before. The platform elongated the leg, providing a touch of elegance, but also lifted the foot out of the hot sand. This was an echo of the patten, one of the earliest conceptions of a platform shoe and worn in the fifteenth century as a way of lifting its wearer above the refuse, sewage and manure with which most streets were littered. By the seventeenth century, the well-to-do of Italy and Spain wore their towering *chopines* under floor-length skirts simply as a means of exaggerating their height.

Above: A platform in golden kid multi-coloured suede and a cork heel, designed for the American star Judy Garland by Salvatore Ferragamo in 1938.

As platforms found practical popularity on the beaches of the USA, such designers as Roger Vivier, Elsa Schiaparelli and Ferragamo explored their fashionability. Yet it was not until the early years of the 1940s that platforms became a widespread fashion choice, the wall of the platform giving ample room for various forms of decoration, from appliqué to tassels. Some attribute this to the rise to stardom of five-foot-tall dancer and singer Carmen Miranda – aka The Brazilian Bombshell – who was Hollywood's highest-paid entertainer by 1945 and who made platform shoes (often by Ferragamo) a signature style. But, while the USA saw the platform as glamorous, it was more necessity that drove the look elsewhere. In war-torn Europe, and especially in occupied France, a lack of leather for soles or components for heels saw women adopt a wooden platform as a plentiful alternative. Shortages, similarly, were said to have prompted Ferragamo's first experiments with high cork soles in Italy during the 1930s.

The platform would, periodically, be revisited by fashion. Biba's Barbara Hulanicki introduced a platform boot in 1968, while British shoe designer Terry DeHavilland helped make the platform as much part of the iconography of the 1970s as the 1940s, especially since his vertiginous versions for Bianca Jagger and Angie and David Bowie were so outrageous. Platforms returned again in the 1990s, when a thick sole was found on all styles of footwear, from black fetishistic boots to clogs and from brothel creepers to sneakers, mainly thanks to Vivienne Westwood. In 1993, model Naomi Campbell tumbled while on the catwalk for Westwood wearing her blue, 25cm (10 inch) Super Elevated Gillie shoes.

Right: The doyenne of the platform shoe, actress and dancer Carmen Miranda, in 1947.
Below: A single platform shoe, complete with back-stage paass to the 1975 Rolling Stones tour of the USA – as worn by Bianca Jagger.

BALLET PUMP

The ballet pump is typically regarded as pirouetting from stage to catwalk during the 1940s and 1950s. It was in 1944, towards the end of World War II, that the pioneering American casualwear designer Claire McCardell asked the New York-based ballet shoemaker Capezio to create a version robust enough to be worn outside. McCardell christened the style 'ballerinas' and soon had a hit on her hands. It was a supremely comfortable shoe whose simplicity meant it could be worn with almost anything and, crucially, it could be made without the restrictions imposed by wartime rationing. Indeed, ballet pumps were exempt. Such was the success of the style that, by the following decade, the ballet flat was the definitive shoe choice of teenage girls, especially as its thin sole and super-soft flexible upper allowed easy movement for the dance crazes that accompanied both big band and fledgling rock'n'roll music.

As with many fashion staples, it was cinema, however, that cemented the ballet pump within the womenswear canon. Audrey Hepburn – whose influence made the little black dress (see p.42), white shirt and Capri-style pants (see p.98) important fashions too – adopted the shoe for a number of her biggest films, including *Roman Holiday* (William Wyler, 1953), *Sabrina* (Billy Wilder, 1954) and *Funny Face* (Stanley Donen, 1957). Hepburn, interestingly, had once been a ballet dancer herself. But perhaps the bigger contribution to its success was the decision of the costumier for Roger Vadim's film *And God Created Woman* (1956) to dress its star, Brigitte Bardot, in a pair. Specifically, a pair made for her in red lambskin with a front tie by Parisian ballet shoemaker Rose Repetto, since the late 1940s the choice of professional dancers. This gave what had come to be perceived as a girlish, gamine shoe a new sexiness. Come the 1960s, the ballet pump was the easy choice to wear with pedal pushers, or, decades later, dresses or jeans.

Opposite: Audrey Hepburn in a studio shot to promote *Sabrina* in 1954, the film that first associated her with the ballet pump.
Below: Brigitte Bardot in ballet pumps in a still from *And God Created Woman* (1956).

The ballet pump's uptake as a fashion item, however, does not simply owe a debt to ballet. It is equally true that the modern conception of the ballet shoe – heel-less, unlike the earliest ballet shoes worn at France's Académie Royale de Danse from 1681 – owes a debt to fashion. For roughly half a century from the late 1700s, a silk slipper-like shoe much like the ballet pump in its cut and simplicity (with perhaps a ribbon fastening for the ankle or, later, a strip of elastic) was the day-to-day choice of any fashionable Western European woman, the only fashion variation being in changes to toe shape, whether rounded or more pointed.

Repetto has gone on to become one of the world's most prestigious producers of ballet pumps, and, in 2011, it launched an atelier service in London's Selfridges department store, whereby customers can design their own ballet flat, and a bespoke pair is made at the firm's factory in France. The brand still uses the same stitching techniques found on traditional pointe shoes to make a strong toe seam.

From the pale pink shades to the two-tone style introduced by Chanel, ballet pumps are timeless, as Calgary Avansino, *Vogue*'s executive fashion director, states: 'It is very rare in the fashion world – the ballet pump has the unique trait of combining comfort and ease with class and style.'

Opposite top: Brigitte Bardot wearing her trademark ballet pumps in 1962.
Opposite bottom: Some of the many hues of ballet pumps from the dancewear company Repetto.
Right: First Lady Michelle Obama in yellow pumps with President Obama in Florida in 2010.

RIDING BOOT

Shoe designer Christian Louboutin was not the first to paint a sole red. Mongol tribesmen painted the heels of their boots red, and it is possible to attribute the invention of the heel for riding to the Mongols of the thirteenth and fourteenth centuries (their period of empire-building). As with the cowboy boot (see p.175), the toe was pointed, better to go through a stirrup, while the heel of the boot was higher than typical and angled towards the toe, giving a purchase on a stirrup while preventing the shoe from slipping right through it. These then, might be considered the first riding boots, and subsequent styles were an equal mix of function and panache: riding boots of early-seventeenth-century Western Europe, for example, had the same 5cm (2 inch) heel, pointed last and straight soles (meaning that either boot could be worn on either foot, allowing wear to be more evenly distributed), but the shaft flared at the top of the thigh. They were as dramatic and piratical as they were practical.

Some women wore various styles of boot for riding during this and the eighteenth century, though it was not at all uncommon for them to wear shoes or ankle boots of some kind. Yet, it was not until the early nineteenth century that boots became fashionable, in particular for women, despite their association with nobility, generally the only people wealthy enough to own a mount. War may have provided the turning point, with the 1815 victory of Arthur Wellesley, 1st Duke of Wellington, over Napoleon Bonaparte at the Battle of Waterloo prompting in the UK a national trend for what was deemed the Wellington boot – with a low heel and mid-calf shaft, these were made of leather, not the rubber of the twentieth-century wellie.

By the 1850s, the two-piece Wellington boot, known as a Full Wellington, had become standard issue for military men, adding to the style's glamour. Equestrian boots for women often came with a

Opposite: A spats-style button-up riding boot, shot for a fashion editorial during the 1960s. Below:Two-tone riding boots by Pierre Cardin worn Cossack-style with trousers tucked in, in 1972.

field-boot closure, lacing like a corset from the top of the vamp and up the lower part of the shaft, making them considerably easier to put on in a ladylike fashion.

Womenswear continued to experiment with various heights of boot from then onwards; ankle boots, for example, had been worn for walking as an outdoor pursuit since the late 1780s, but would in turn become the side-laced Adelaides of the 1830s (named after King William IV's queen consort), the button-fronted boots of the 1880s, through to designers Pierre Cardin and André Courrèges's modish go-go boots of the 1960s.

But, any boot that could really claim to be a riding boot would derive from the initial Wellington style. Often practicality was at the root of the choice; the high boot underwent a resurgence in the 1890s, for example, when bicycling became fashionable for women and a boot was required to protect their stockings, while the vogue for the close-fitting, pull-on, knee-high Russian boots of the early 1920s were regarded as a more chic, leather alternative to galoshes or rain boots, and were originally designed for his wife by couturier Paul Poiret.

The riding-boot style soon superseded necessity. Russian boots prefigured the types of boot that would be termed young and modern in the 1960s, thanks in large part to those designed by Balenciaga and Roger Vivier for Yves Saint Laurent, which would be hailed as more progressive, capable alternatives to the post-war ladylike and dainty fashion attributed to Christian Dior's New Look. It is perhaps ironic that it was the practical, masculine nature of the tall boot that in the end made it so fashionable for women.

Opposite: Barbara Allen and Jerry Hall in Gucci riding boots and other riding-inspired garb in 1978.
Below right: Princess Anne, Olympic equestrian, at the Montreal Games in 1976.
Below right: Riding boots found new popularity when bicycle riding became the new fad of the late nineteenth century.

SANDAL

'The time of the fable is over, the Reign of History is beginning.' Such was Josephine Bonaparte's admonishment to society beauty Madame Tallien and two friends whose excessive dress, she warned them, would not be tolerated again. And when the wife of the Emperor of France criticizes one's clothing, one might well take note. These women's offence? In 1799, they appeared at a state function wearing tunics and, what seemed to fuel the furore, sandals with purple straps. For good measure, they wore rings on their exposed toes.

Such things might have been acceptable portrayed in art, inspired as it was at the time by the taste for classicism and the style of ancient Greek and Roman statuary. But, to wear open-toed sandals in real life was a step too far. The solution, it turned out, was to create the illusion of doing so, by painting straps and cut-outs over a closed shoe and using an underlay matched to coloured stockings. Come 1800 – and even though the sandal style had, in effect, been worn for tens of thousands of years, tying a protective leather layer to the sole being one of the most basic ways of creating a shoe – the term 'sandal' meant just that: any closed shoe with laces that crossed over the instep and tied around the ankle.

Remarkably, it was not until 1907 that the sandal in its modern (or rather ancient) conception – a shoe held on with straps that exposed the feet and toes – entered fashion, and then tentatively. Ahead of her time, that year the French couturier Madeleine Vionnet showed her models wearing sandals, but it would not be until the 1920s that the shoe form became widely acceptable, and then mainly as a practical style to wear at the beach or the new seaside resorts.

One reason for its appeal was the new fashion, popularized by Coco Chanel, for having a tan. Traditional bathing shoes covered the instep

Opposite: American singer Carly Simon in knee-high Roman sandals, in the New York summer of 1971.
Below left: Norwegian actress Greta Gynt models wooden-soled sandals for Clarks in the 1940s.
Below right: An 18-carat-gold sandal by Salvatore Ferragamo, produced in 1956.

Photographer John Hinde uses the magnificent facade of Wells Cathedral as a backcloth to lovely Greta Gynt—latest star discovered by Two Cities films— Miss Gynt herself has discovered Clarks latest wood-soled sandals —the finishing touch to a carefree summer outfit.

Made by C. & J. CLARK, LTD. (wholesale only) and by Clarks (Ireland) Ltd., Dundalk.

Clarks

and created a tan line around the ankle. The platform style that followed originated as a beach sandal, too, its thick sole designed to sink into the sand allowing the foot to remain protected above it. By the 1930s, the basic sandal might be worn for eveningwear, but only styles with a closed toe, and only worn with stockings. To have bare legs at this time was deemed almost as unacceptable as exposing one's toes in Napoleonic France.

The sandal might be said to have lived a double life: while some were getting dressier, others were becoming much more basic. One theory has it that the demand for the latter was due to their being worn by Hollywood starlets off-set, who in turn had been introduced to them through the spate of biblical epics filmed during the pre-World War II years. Cecil B. DeMille, the director behind many of these, had, after all, hired shoe designer Salvatore Ferragamo to make the footwear as authentic as possible, an ethos that would similarly appeal to sandal-wearing hippies in the 1960s.

War helped the sandal's progress: shortages encouraged minimal use of leather wherever possible and the style became the shoe of choice for the pin-ups, both photographed and, more typically, as illustrated by the likes of Alberto Vargas and George Petty. These sassy girls – role models of a sort – underpinned the sexiness of the sandal, with its 'peekaboo' style and the notion of 'toe cleavage', only made more popular by the advent of colourful nail varnish. The Empress Josephine would not have been amused.

**Below: A model on the beach showing off patriotic fashions in the USA in 1941.
Opposite: Playing cards featuring classic illustrated pin-ups by the artist Alberto Vargas, produced in 1946.**

PLIMSOLL

The ancestor of what by the 1980s had become the ubiquitous and unisex trainer, or sneaker in the USA, was designed for a much more sedate purpose: walking on the beach. The original plimsoll was a product of mid-to-late-nineteenth-century British seaside holidays, and the discovery by working men that their sturdy boots were inappropriate for the setting and the sand alike. The result was an uptake of the 'sand shoe', a new, cheap, lightweight shoe with a cool, fast-drying canvas upper and rubber sole, popularized by the Liverpool Rubber Company (established 1861 and later bought by Dunlop). The sole was secured to the canvas by way of a rubber strip that gave the shoe its name, echoing as it did the white Plimsoll line introduced in 1876 to indicate the maximum depth to which a ship's hull might be immersed when loaded with cargo. The seafaring analogy was particularly apt given its typical beach use.

The shoe was soon being worn by women and the sporty, proving itself ideal for court sports due to the cushioning and grip it provided and the protection it afforded the playing surface. Yachtsmen and women appreciated the plimsoll for similar reasons, while the armed services made them part of standard issue kit for use during PT, or physical training. Advances in the design saw the addition of a rubber toecap to prevent the big toe wearing through the canvas, and the first instances of branded plimsoll-type footwear began to appear.

Most notably, 1908 saw the founding of the Converse Rubber Shoe Company, based in Malden, Massachusetts. The company quickly established a firm reputation making rubber-soled shoes, breaking into the tennis shoe market in 1915 and launching the Converse All-Star basketball shoe in 1917. A boot followed when company salesman and ex-basketball star Charles, or 'Chuck', Taylor suggested the addition of a patch to protect the ankle. The boot became the staple footwear for college sports in the USA for many decades, and was only available in black until 1947, when a white version was introduced. This fast became part of the uniform of the American teenager of the 1950s, along with white T-shirts and a pair of Levi's.

By 1966, the Converse take on the plimsoll had become the firm market leader, and seven colour options were introduced. This heralded the era of bold, bright sneaker design – from companies such as New Balance and Nike – made possible by the synthetic fabrics available, and the designs became more cultish and collectible.

From the 1970s onwards, there was an increased availability of sports shoes designed for specific activities and much more outlandish styling, thanks in part to the technical advances made possible by new materials. Fashion, however, remained fond of the minimalistic simplicity of the plimsoll, and the way that, like denim, it improved aesthetically with age. The plimsoll formed a stylistic component of key, often music-led, subcultures from the late 1970s onwards, including American punk rock, grunge (worn with a floral dress and outsized cardigan), American West Coast hip-hop and hardcore punk/emo as well as many others with a retro leaning. Then, the plimsoll's often short shelf-life – scuffs, dirt and holes – only added to its appeal. In the 2010s, when its back-to-basics design and near disposability saw it dubbed the 'Shoreditch slipper' (after the then fashionable area of East London), versions from the likes of Keds, Superga, Vans, as well as brand-free traditional school plimsolls, were teamed with rolled-up jeans and tea-dresses.

Below: American actress Katharine Hepburn in white tennis plimsolls, posing with Donald Budge for a publicity shot in 1952.
Opposite: Swiss-American actress Ursula Andress, in baseball jacket and matching plimsolls, in 1978.

COWBOY BOOT

The cowboy boot is sometimes perceived as being a largely decorative form of bygone dress with its rococo shape, highly ornate leatherwork and, of course, more than a hint of the nineteenth-century American Wild West about it. It was during Hollywood's efforts in the 1930s to turn the mythology of the cowboy into cinematic gold – initially through actors like Gene Autry and Roy Rogers – that the cowboy boot was first worn for fashion. Yet, almost everything about the boot, which was originally worn by men and women alike, was shaped by consideration for its function while riding a horse.

The heel was made high, at 5 to 8cms (2 to 3 inches), large and angled towards the instep to help the foot stay in the stirrups, but to prevent it from passing all the way through them. It also dug into the ground when the cowboy or girl wearing them had to restrain or pull back on a wayward horse. Meanwhile, the toe was more chiselled to make it easier to get the foot into the stirrups when mounting a horse. The boot's wide opening and lack of lacing not only made it easier to get on while wearing heavy-duty all-weather clothes, but also made it easier to free the foot from the boot and stirrup if thrown from the horse. A tight-fitting vamp kept the boot secure on the foot while upright. The height of the main part was selected to protect the rider's legs from stones, brambles and the like (the shorter, so-called Roper, version of the cowboy boot came in with rodeo, since rodeo riders had to be free to ride but also to run after and rope a calf).

As for the decoration, that was merely an imaginative response to the fact that cowboy boots are stitched on the outside in order that no seams are left to rub against the foot or leg on the inside. The more ornate take on the boot, with inlays and overlays of boldly patterned and coloured leathers, only arrived on later styles of boot from the 1920s onwards. This was when boots began to be worn for show as

Opposite: American actress Raquel Welch dons patriotic bikini and cowboy boots in a promotional shot for the film *Myra Breckinridge*, in 1970.
Below left: The cover of *Life* magazine in 1940 shows the latest teenage fashion – western style.
Below right: Cowboy boots for sale at Libertad Market, in Guadalajara, Mexico.

much as for work; rodeo blended ranch skills with entertainment, while Hollywood sought to give its big-screen cowboys – and, eventually, cowgirls such as the B-movie favourite Yvonne De Carlo – ever more spectacle.

Hollywood had a lasting effect on the appeal of the boot, encouraging its embrace as a symbol of American history and of heroic individualism, much as it did with denims. Marilyn Monroe posed in cowboy boots, in some early shots wearing little else bar a Stetson, in keeping with the illustrated pin-ups of the period. By the 1960s, they had become a fashion staple, backed by the rising popularity of Country and Western music and the boot being worn by stars like Dolly Parton. By the 1990s they were ripe for reinterpretation, worn around town, found to be useful at muddy music festivals and as likely to be seen on Britney Spears, Jessica Simpson or Kate Moss as anyone near a horse. And again in the 2010s the boot made a fashionable return with designers such as Marc Jacobs and Balmain creating styles for women in metallics, black velvet or black-and-white co-respondent designs.

Remarkably, given the level of consideration and innovation that went into the cowboy boot, who invented them has escaped record. It has been suggested that the style probably originated in either Texas or Kansas and a forerunner was Kansas's Hyer Boot Company, established by Charles and Edward Hyer after taking on their German immigrant father William's shoemaking business in 1880. However, ancient cultures in which the horse figured highly also wore similar footwear. The fifth-century Huns of central Asia may have passed on their designs to the Moors, who took them to Spain, with the Spanish then exporting the style to the New World via Mexico and California, becoming, in effect, the first cowboys, the *vaqueros*.

American journalist Louise Bryant poses in Russian costume, complete with western cowboy boots, in 1918.

Above: American singer Alicia Keyes, snapped on the street in New York in 2006.
Right: A pair of the many high-heeled cowboy boots owned by American Country & Western legend Dolly Parton.

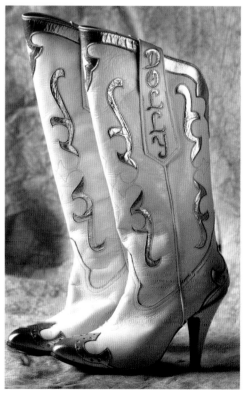

KITTEN HEEL

If the stiletto (see p.153) of the 1950s suggested sex, soon a more respectable heel would be in demand – still a heel, but sweeter, maybe even girlish. The name kitten heel, after all, came from period slang for a young, inexperienced girl for whom a short, tapered heel, between 3.5 and 5 cms (1½ and 2 inches) high, supported by a metal internal stem safely situated right in the middle of the heel, would be an appropriate starter heel before graduating on to more towering footwear. In fact, some USA shoe retailers referred to the kitten heel as the 'trainer heel'.

The rival stiletto was also something of a statement – fashion and otherwise – that not all young women wanted to make so soon after the model's introduction. Yes, teenage girls quickly embraced the kitten heel in the expectation that they might one day move on to higher things. But, many adult women began to wear them, too, regarding them as a compromise between the extremes of crippling stilettos and inelegant, childish flats.

The kitten heel typically came with a pointed toe, but its chief characteristic – the dainty heel – meant that, unlike its taller cousin, it left most wearers considerably more mobile, and with less of a sassy walk to boot. Sometimes, its height was part of its appeal in a more complex way: by keeping women more diminutive in relation to men and so suggesting youth and innocence. And, as heel height had been used since medieval times, it also spoke of status and power. Oscar-winning costumier Edith Head selected a pair of kitten heels for Audrey Hepburn to wear in *Sabrina* (Billy Wilder, 1954) opposite Humphrey Bogart, to ensure they did not stand eye to eye; the kitten heel, consequently, became known as the 'Sabrina heel'. Hepburn, who came to be associated with the style (as well as the ballet pump, see p.159), also wore them a few years later in *Funny Face* (Stanley Donen, 1957), opposite Fred Astaire. In both instances, the shoes were by Salvatore Ferragamo, the Italian shoe designer whom Hepburn met while living in Rome to shoot *Roman Holiday* (William Wyler, 1953), and to whose shoes she became a life-long devotee.

During the 1960s, the kitten heel went 'toe to toe' with the stiletto as the grown woman's shoe of choice, the latter attracting increased criticism from the era's burgeoning women's liberation movement, before more radical styles such as the platform (see p.156) returned in force during the 1970s. But, the kitten heel's practicality meant it never quite disappeared, even if it battled with its image of being rather prim and ladylike. However, it was for this reason that it became popular in the 1980s as more women found themselves needing to dress for executive positions in the workplace. And, again during the 2000s and 2010s, the style proved ideal for 'first ladies', from the USA's Michelle Obama to France's Carla Bruni; the kitten heel expressed femininity but not the inappropriate femme fatale.

Below: Carla Bruni-Sarkozy, snapped in Christian Louboutin kitten heels at the Elysée Palace in Paris in 2010.
Opposite: The film poster for the Italian release of *Breakfast at Tiffany's* (1961), with Audrey Hepburn in kitten heels.

PEEP-TOE & SLING-BACK

If the Victorian gentlewoman was careful, as propriety dictated, to expose a minimum of bare skin in her dress, leading to the Victorian gentleman famously palpitating at the sight of a bare ankle, such concerns, one might imagine, would be long out of date come 1938. But the vogue for open-toed and slingback shoes – both styles a version of the standard pump (see p.159) and both largely down to Italian shoe designer Salvatore Ferragamo – provoked controversy when they came out in that year. The slingback is a backless shoe, characterized by a strap that crosses behind the heel or ankle, while the peep-toe has an opening at the front of the shoe to allow the toes to show. This was an era when bare legs away from beach or sport were simply not done, yet both styles of shoe, the slingback in particular, were hard to wear with stockings because the heel tended to slip out and because stockings of the time still had unsightly reinforced toes and heels.

In 1939, the editor of American *Vogue* railed against the slingback: 'From the beginning of this fashion I have felt it was a distinctly bad style. You [the shoe industry] have gotten women almost barefooted now.' The industry responded in some small way: peep-toes were made smaller and strips added to heel straps on slingbacks to hide the reinforced part of stockings. But neither the slingback nor the peep-toe went away, even if slingbacks tended to be worn only at the beach or as part of formal eveningwear, when a long dress largely hid the shoe anyway. By the 1940s, stocking manufacturers came up with a solution: the launch of stockings without the obviously reinforced heel or toe.

It was just as well. Both peep-toes and slingbacks became styles that defined the much less conservative, post-war 1940s, gracing the feet of Hollywood starlets from Greta Garbo to Joan Crawford and from Anne Miller to Carmen Miranda (leading exponent of the platform peep-toe), and becoming notably sexualized objects in the process. Indeed, it was Ferragamo's work with costume departments at Hollywood studios that helped ensure these shoes were the styles of the era's bombshells and pin-up girls.

Ironically, given the initial controversy, what appealed to many designers and their customers about the slingback especially was not only that it could be slipped on and off without needing to actually undo the heel-strap buckle, but that this strap so secured the shoe to the foot that it allowed more of the upper to be coyly (and not so coyly) cut away, thus exposing more of the foot. This also encouraged the use of new synthetic materials in brighter colours and unusual finishes, in itself an added bonus in the face of post-war leather shortages. As one Sears Roebuck advertisement of the era had it: 'Backless Beauties in Butterfly Colors – Pastels, new and terrific ... or in rich, deeper hues.... Light, graceful, they make the most of pretty feet, the least of summer temperatures.'

Below: Black leather peep-toe pumps from French shoe designer Christian Louboutin's 2009 collection.
Opposite: Actress Jane Birkin in platform-soled slingbacks, in 1973.

WEDGE

Many styles of shoe date back centuries; such has been the symbolism of the shoe in courtly life that radical experimentation in shoemaking means that even the most extreme designs are often much older than might be imagined. But the wedge, the more accessible forebear of the towering platform (see p.156), can be dated to 1936 and a look created by Italian designer Salvatore Ferragamo. He filled the space between a shoe's traditional block heel and its sole, extending the heel so it ran under the foot. The use of wood made the shoe solid and inexpensive, and his first designs comprised two pieces of wood that produced an F-shaped curve in the back of the heel. Later, the use of layered cork created wedges that offered both previous advantages while also being light. The fashion press helped promote their appeal; *Harper's Bazaar* in 1938 noted that 'Italian women [in particular] have literally gone mad for them', though offered no evidence to explain whether it really meant the unlikely scenario of a shoe style prompting insanity.

The style's qualities were to become important the following year with the outbreak of World War II and the introduction of rationing. In fact, it was the imposition of rationing that gave the wedge some of its more unusual treatments. The wedge in suede became fashionable because suede was considered suitable for formal and informal wear and also because it allowed the use of less high-quality hides (suede being the result of buffing or sanding the imperfections out of these hides). Ironically, perhaps, it also encouraged the use of more exotic skins, the likes of snake, lizard, crocodile and alligator, because they could still be easily imported to the USA from South America (largely unaffected by the war), and because they were deemed of no use to the war effort. In the USA, where materials were more widely available, the wall of a wedge might be wrapped in linen or raffia, espadrille style.

A solid, balanced shoe, the wedge also found popularity during this period as more people were walking or using public transport because most private cars had been co-opted for the war effort or were too expensive to run. The wedge answered the call for the stylish but practical. That Ferragamo had in 1939 created a pair – the sole of which comprised multicoloured fabric layers – for Judy Garland, then one of the world's biggest stars, only helped to ensure its fame. By the time publicity shots caught a bikini-clad Marilyn Monroe wearing them poolside in 1950, the wedge, which elongated the leg without being uncomfortable to walk in, was well established as a wardrobe staple.

The wedge enjoyed bouts of fashionability over the coming decades. In the 1970s, for example, and again in the 2010s. While the idea for hidden lifts was not a new one – a patent for the design was filed in the USA by C. O. Christy in 1952, and athletic footwear companies had unsuccessfully also tried to launch styles using them in the 1990s – it took French designer Isabel Marant to spark a trend. She showed her Spring/Summer 2012 catwalk models wearing Nike Air Force 1-style sneakers with what might be called an internal wedge, and was quickly and widely copied, with other companies applying the idea to many sorts of shoe. 'It's something I did since I was a teenager: I would cut up cork and put pieces into my trainers because I wanted to look taller,' the designer noted. 'Sneakers are comfortable but at the same time not very elegant. To have a little heel in it makes a difference, it gives you legs.'

Above: A platform sneaker by Wanted, 2013.
Below: The patent application for a wedge – 'shoes with lifted heel but without stiletto heel' – filed by Salvatore Ferragamo in December 1937.
Opposite: Street style in wedges, Berlin, 2014.

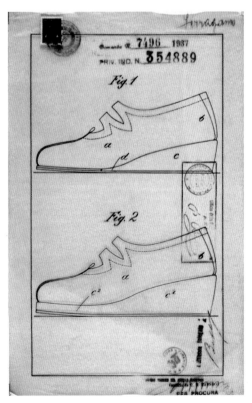

9.

ACCESSORIES

silk scarf / cloche / costume jewellery / it bag / beret

SILK SCARF

The scarf can be worn in many ways: around the neck, as a shawl, around or over the head or as an observance of religious direction – historically Christian women wore wimples, today married Jewish women wear a *tichel* and some Muslim women a hijab. The scarf also has a practical use worn this way, to protect and to provide warmth.

However, the scarf, particularly the printed silk scarf, has connotations of a certain style, and in some cultures a certain class. Worn over the head and tied under the chin in babushka fashion – after the Russian for 'grandmother' – it could denote seniority in Eastern Europe, or upper-class or even aristocratic leanings in Western Europe. Queen Victoria did much to popularize the wearing of then novel accessories such as scarves, the quality and colour of which were used as distinct means of class differentiation. Not for nothing is one of the most celebrated headscarf-wearers Queen Elizabeth II.

While head and neck scarves have been worn since ancient Egyptian times – images of Queen Nefertiti show her wearing a headscarf under a headdress – and throughout the Middle Ages, in the modern era they have also been regarded as fashion items. Napoleon Bonaparte helped spark a trend for them by sending cashmere scarves (by the dozen) back to his empress, Josephine, while American, early-twentieth-century modern dance pioneer Isadora Duncan, who popularized the wearing of long flowing scarves, paid the highest price for her style – she died when her scarf became caught up in the wheel of a car and broke her neck ('affectations can be dangerous,' Gertrude Stein noted). This was the golden era of such stores as Liberty of London, whose bold art-nouveau printing found a perfect vehicle in the headscarf.

Liberty scarves, however, were pre-dated by arguably the leading proponent and maker of the most desirable examples of the silk scarf:

Opposite: American film star Faye Dunaway in a still from the film *Bonnie and Clyde* (1967), set in the 1930s.
Below left: American actress Gene Tierney ensures her headscarf matches both swimsuit and big cat, in 1954.
Below right: A selection of silk scarves from one of the world's most famed makers, Hermès.

Above: British model Twiggy, in matching
scarf and eye-shadow, in 1970.

French company Hermès. It launched its first '*carré*', as it refers to its square-shaped scarves, in 1937 under the direction of Robert Dumas Hermès, with a print illustrating the inauguration of the Parisian Madeleine-to-Bastille bus line (indeed, scarves were often created and bought as souvenirs). The company went on to commission artists from Cassandre to Jean-Louis Clerc to design its collectible, 90cm-square (35 inches), silk twill *carrés*.

But the scarf's history was not all silky smooth. The invention of rayon as a staple fibre in the 1920s made more inventive printing and a more affordable price possible. By the 1950s, the scarf was in its heyday, regarded as colourful but demure and, perhaps above all, ladylike – all characteristics that could be applied to wearers Grace Kelly, Elizabeth Taylor and Audrey Hepburn. 'When I wear a silk scarf I never feel so definitely like a woman, a beautiful woman,' Hepburn once said.

However, those same traits did not suit the sexual revolution and gender politics of the 1960s, in spite of the far from conservative prints available from such designers as Elsa Schiaparelli. During the following decade, it took the first applications of designer logos, a new modernism in prints and a reappraisal of the scarf as something else entirely (something that could be worn creatively, as a belt or even tied around the torso as a kind of bandeau top) for it to be revived. By the twenty-first century, new digital-printing technology gave a further lease of life to the silk scarf, but rarely was it worn babushka-style, the Queen of England aside.

American actress Janet Leigh wearing a floral silk scarf, in the late 1960s.

CLOCHE

Few hats are as synonymous with an era as the cloche, which takes its name from the French word for bell. This simple felt construction, initially made by a milliner placing a sheet of felt over a client's head and cutting and folding it to fit in a bell-like shape, is emblematic of the 1920s. The hat was the invention of self-taught French milliner Caroline Reboux around 1908, whose Paris shop was the haunt of the period's trend-setting celebrities including Marlene Dietrich and, later, Wallis Simpson. It was Reboux who also helped to popularize the other headwear that defined the decade: the lamé turban and hats worn with a veil. Several hundred of Reboux's designs are held at the Musée de la Mode et du Textile in Paris.

Well established by 1916, the cloche was designed to be worn low on the forehead, affording a degree of protection and privacy, which by turns suggested a certain shyness and a certain hauteur. Wearers had to hold their head high to see where they were going, a pose of pride that also suited the emancipation of women then afoot. 'There's a mystery to the cloche,' as Mark Bridges has noted. 'They sort of half hide the face and are coy.' Bridges, the costume designer for the Oscar-winning movie *The Artist* (Michel Hazanavicius, 2011), was not alone in his use of the cloche to signal a specific moment in time; such movies as *The Boy Friend* (Ken Russell, 1971) and *The Changeling* (Clint Eastwood, 2008) also appreciated the fact.

The style originated with a broader-brimmed model. With each evolution of her design, Reboux cut the brim away more and more to create an almost rimless, jauntier, more streamlined and decidedly modern model. The cloche freed its wearer from the weight and inconvenience of the outsize, overly ornate hat styles of the Victorian era. But it was still made distinctive through its decoration, which, after 1925, followed the decade's art-deco influence: appliqué, brooches, embroidery and the like, typically only on one side of the hat. The well-off would also pick models with complex construction techniques such as zigzag seaming. While felt had the advantage of being easily moulded, allowing the basic cloche to be affordably mass-produced, more expensive models in silk, horsehair, beads, lace and bamboo also appeared. One cloche, made for the London department store Liberty in 1928 and designed to be worn at a wedding, came with blue ostrich feathers and was lined in silk taffeta.

The style also worked well with the era's shorter hairstyles, in keeping with fashion's more boyish, less figure-hugging shapes. The short bob hairstyle originated around 1926, and was said to have been inspired by the shape of the cloche. Certainly, silent movie superstar Louise Brooks, whose trademark bob popularized the cut, also wore cloches throughout her career. Such couture houses as Lanvin even opened ateliers to produce cloches that matched their clothing designs.

By the end of the 1920s, there was a trend to turn up the brims of the hat, which lasted until the return of more elaborate hairstyles towards the end of the decade, which ensured that the cloche had fallen out of fashion by the mid-1930s. It has reappeared since – during the 1960s and then again with Patrick Kelly's buttoned-brim version in the 1980s, and even in 2007 when *Elle* magazine termed it 'the haute accessory of the moment'.

Above: American actress Angelina Jolie in the film *The Changeling* (2008)
Opposite: A young Marlene Dietrich in the archetypal 'flapper' style of the 1920s.

French couturière Coco Chanel, in her
signature string of pearls, in 1936.

COSTUME JEWELLERY

In some ways, costume jewellery was the forerunner of fast fashion. Jewellery had, for generations, been intended to be passed down through the generations; it was by definition precious and timeless, and this was reflected in the materials used and craft employed to make it. Costume jewellery, its name reflecting the use of the word 'costume' to refer to what we now call an 'outfit', was meant to be as short-lived as the clothing style it was designed to complement.

Czechoslovakia became the world leader in costume jewellery production in the 1930s. But, it was not necessarily about being cheap. Affordable jewellery had, in fact, been made since the eighteenth century using glass, paste and base metals to look like gems and gold. By the nineteenth century, with an emerging middle class, there was also new demand for an accessible but not imitation product, resulting in an increase in production using, for example, semi-precious stones and rolled gold. Both types were, however, still considered as jewellery to be worn throughout one's life. Not so costume jewellery; like clothing, it went out of date and needed replacing.

Among the earlier twentieth-century designs are those ascribed to Coco Chanel during the 1920s. She produced pieces in faux pearls, encouraging the string of pearls to be worn as a fashion, and making them a signature style for herself to boot. Other designers sought to make the most of the graphic designs then popular thanks to the art-deco movement, which was itself in part about marrying artistry with mass production. Jewellery quickly moved from being sensuously curvaceous to boldly geometric. But through the 1930s, and especially with the outbreak of World War II in 1939 which destroyed much of the European costume-jewellery business and saw many of its designers emigrate to the USA, a more American mood, blending Hollywood glamour with new unexpected materials, became prevalent.

A 'Palm Beach' brooch designed by Kenneth Jay Lane in 2011 and worth just $100.

Top: Italian socialite Principessa Luciana Pignatelli in a bejewelled collar and tube top by Tiziani Boutique in 1966.
Bottom: American actress Grace Kelly in a still from the film *To Catch a Thief* (1955).

Add in the pressures of the war, during which time rapid changes in fashion were few and clothing had to last, and the appeal to regularly update an outfit with new jewellery was only heightened. As *The New York Times* put it in 1943: 'Designers have rallied valiantly and have evolved various ingenious creations from non-priority materials. Everything from spaghetti to cloth dipped in wax is utilized for beautiful or amusing gadgets [jewellery], to add an individual touch to the simplest of suits and dresses.' Acetate was treated to look like sparkling stones, plastic polished to simulate 'berries glistening with dew', paper added, silvered or made clear and embedded with ceramics. Leather, wood, seashells, straw, wool, fabric and moulded glass were all used. The spaghetti, by the way, was coloured, fixed and twisted into rope necklaces then dried so that it never went doughy.

So high was the turnover of fashions in costume jewellery that, from the 1940s, some companies offered make-it-yourself kits. One Chicago maker, Flower Materials, launched a scheme whereby people could make costume jewellery in their spare time to sell to friends. 'All you do is select the mounting for a ring, necklace or bracelet and add the lustrous beauty of opulently colored stones, gleaming rhinestones or majestic pearls,' explained its 1951 catalogue, 'And the results – stunning costume jewelry made with your own hands that looks so much like real expensive jewellery that you'll be proud to wear it.'

Far from being considered a poor man's alternative, costume jewellery soon developed a prestige in its own right: not just through the name Chanel, but also Pennino, Sphinx, Crown Trifari, Lisner, Miriam Haskell, Kim Craftsmen and Kenneth Jay Lane. Costume jewellery, after all, was a product the movie stars of the period, notably Jane Russell, Vivien Leigh and Elizabeth Taylor, were happy both to wear and to put their names to in advertisements. Kenneth Jay Lane made one-off designs for the likes of Audrey Hepburn and Jacqueline Kennedy Onassis.

The accessibility of costume jewellery encouraged both more outlandish design and changes to the way in which jewellery was worn. Rather than a single, eye-catching piece, costume jewellery was piled on: a dozen bracelets on one arm, multiple necklaces of all lengths and outsize earrings. 'This winter may go down in fashion history as the time when the old term of contempt, "she's done up like a Christmas tree," became a compliment,' noted one 1951 US article. Since costume jewellery's accessibility also brought with it the idea of novelty, a pair of Christmas tree earrings was duly produced.

Model Suzy Parker in a fake moonstone
necklace and earrings by Miriam Haskell in
1957.

IT BAG

Whether or not it can be called the definitive 'it bag' – the fashion-industry term from the 1990s for a high-priced designer handbag and borrowed from the 'it girl' reference to Clara Bow in the 1927 silent movie *It* – the Hermès Kelly bag took a curious road to fame. Designed in 1923 by Emile-Maurice Hermès and Ettore Bugatti (of the Italian car-makers), the bag was based on an 1892 saddle holder known as the *Haut à Courroies* (bag with tall handles). It was updated again during the 1930s by Robert Dumas, Hermès's son-in-law, as a spacious travel bag called a *sac à dépêche*. But, it first came to prominence in Alfred Hitchcock's *To Catch a Thief* (1955) when costumier Edith Head selected it for Grace Kelly to use in her role. The bag, a trapezium closed with two straps, has four studs on the bottom and a single handle, and is sold in eight sizes. The padlock, keys and hardware are made from white or yellow gold, and the construction of each bag takes between 18 and 25 hours.

Grace Kelly used it off set, too. A little over a year later, now married to Prince Rainer III of Monaco, she appeared on the cover of *Life* magazine in 1956. There the bag was: on the lap of the movie star, less as a statement of her good taste or her practicality, and more as a way to hide the fact that she was pregnant. Certainly, Kelly held on tightly to the bag, and so loyally that, although other stars such as Ingrid Bergman and Marlene Dietrich also used one, the bag unofficially took Kelly's name. In 1977, Hermès officially renamed it the 'Kelly bag'. In the interim, it had become both a statement and a status symbol, pioneering the way for bags to say so much more about their 'wearers' than their need to carry lots of stuff. Fashion companies could now pursue the alchemist's dream of turning mere panels of leather into fashion gold – the iconic bag – and many have tried.

Opposite: Grace Kelly, holding the Hermès bag that took her name, in 1956.
Above: A quilted Chanel bag from the A/W 2005/06 collection.
Right: A Gucci 'Bamboo' bag, at the Gucci fashion show of January 2012.

Actress Audrey Hepburn with her signature
Louis Vuitton bag going through customs at an
airport in 1968.

Hermès struck gold again in 1981 when a chance encounter on a flight between actress Jane Birkin and Hermès chairman Jean-Louis Dumas on a flight sparked an idea. When Birkin's straw bag broke, spilling her effects all over the cabin, he determined to produce a roomier version of the Kelly, with double handles and spill-proof flaps, which launched in 1984. Again, Birkin's loyalty to the design (until, at least, she jokingly claimed to be injuring herself by carrying too much all the time) saw it take her name. Sold in a range of hides from ostrich to crocodile, the bag is lined with goat skin and can even be encrusted with diamonds.

Other notable 'it bags' include Louis Vuitton's 'Speedy,' designed in 1932, akin to a traditional doctor's bag and beloved of Audrey Hepburn, who asked the company to devise a smaller version for her; Chanel's 2.55 quilted clutch bag of 1955; Gucci's 'Bamboo' and 'Constance' bags, often seen on the arm of Jacqueline Kennedy Onassis throughout the 1960s; and Fendi's 'Baguette', designed by Silvia Venturini Fendi in 1997 to be carried under the arm like the French loaf of the same name. The list goes on: Prada's black nylon backpack, Chloé's 'Paddington', Mulberry's 'Bayswater' and Bottega Veneta's 'Intrecciato' leather-weave bags, designed by Tomas Maier, a man who once called the whole idea of the 'it bag' 'totally marketed bullshit'.

Perhaps he was right. When handbags first replaced pockets in revolutionary France in the late 1700s, they were referred to by the English (who soon followed the French lead) as 'indispensables', suggesting even then a dependence on these accessories. The French, however, often called them 'ridicules', mocking the attention that women paid them (though increased travel and restrictive dress would, some 50 years on, make them truly practical). But, rightly or wrongly, the waiting lists for 'it bags' in the late twentieth century spoke of their straight, undeniable desirability. Perhaps the benchmark of the 'it bag' was how quickly and extensively counterfeit versions were made available on backstreet markets.

British actress Jane Birkin, with her Hermès 'Birkin' bag, at a fashion show in 2004.

BERET

Often associated with not just menswear but particularly masculine menswear at that, the beret has its origins with Basque fishermen and sheep farmers, a version of similar head coverings that date to the Bronze Age. It also had widespread use as part of undress uniform within the military of many armed forces around the world, the French doing so first, in 1889. It has a somewhat stereotypical association with the French Resistance during World War II, but also has strong links with some of the most iconic men of the second half of the twentieth century: Pablo Picasso, Che Guevara, Dizzy Gillespie, Ernest Hemingway, John Lennon and the figures of the Beat Generation, among others. It is perhaps surprising that the beret, alternately arty, bohemian and revolutionary, should have a place in womenswear at all.

That it does is a testament to its practicality. Traditionally worn in either brown, red or blue, even though black would become the staple, the beret was easy to make in one piece from wool felt, making it affordable and protective. It is rimless and soft with a flat crown, so it is foldable, comfortable and easy to style. And, above all, it is one of the most simple and versatile head coverings. It fits snugly around the head and can be shaped in a variety of ways: pushed to one side, square on the head or jutting forward, among others.

Women, Coco Chanel included, first appreciated the beret's practicality as sportswear during the 1920s, wearing it pulled low much like a cloche (see p.188), a style it would come to replace. By the end of the decade, the hat had sidestepped its historically male and peasant leaning to become a fashion item for women. Most progressively, Marlene Dietrich wore a beret, acquired from milliner Caroline Reboux in Paris, perched over the side of her head as a decorative rather than protective item. Greta Garbo and Jean Harlow wore the style, too. Lauren Bacall wore a beret throughout the 1940s, when the beret became more widespread, in part because it could easily be made in many colours and from crocheted cotton, wool or acrylic fibres. In 1954, hatmakers Kangol advertised that its 'Anglobasque', 'Tambourin' and 'Beret Capette' fashion berets were available in '40 captivating colours'. However, later in the 1950s, and given increasingly intricate hairstyles, the beret had partly fallen out of favour. But, it was revitalized as a symbol of French patriotism; naturally Brigitte Bardot would wear one.

It could be said that it was a movie that helped revive interest in the headpiece beyond France. The beret was one of the key elements of Faye Dunaway's gangster's moll costume in *Bonnie and Clyde* (Arthur Penn, 1967), such that the movie's costume designer Theadora Van Runkle noted that 'the beret was the final culmination of the silhouette (see p.184). In it she combined all the visual elements of elegance and chic. Without the beret it would have been charming, but not the same.' The following year influential British model Twiggy wore one, with 'Swinging London' designer Mary Quant launching a line of berets in 12 pop colours. The beret has become so much the domain of womenswear that *The Guardian* in 2012 advised: 'A beret on a man is ridiculous'.

Top: A beret-clad Twiggy poses in front of a picture of herself during the 1970s.
Bottom: Swedish actress Greta Garbo in a still from the film *As You Desire Me* (1932).

A model posing in a beret by British designer
Mary Quant, in 1967.

FURTHER READING

Blackman, Cally. *100 Years of Fashion*, Laurence King, 2012.

Cumming, Valerie. *Understanding Fashion History*, Batsford, 2011.

The Design Museum. *Fifty Dresses that Changed the World*, Conran 2009.

Dirix, Emmanuelle and Charlotte Fiel. *1940s Fashion: The Definitive Sourcebook*, Goodman Books, 2013.

English, Bonnie. *A Cultural History of Fashion in the 20th and 21st Centuries: From Catwalk to Sidewalk*, 2nd edition, Bloomsbury Academic, 2013.

Fukai, Akiki. *Fashion: A History from the 18th to the 20th Century*, Taschen, 2006.

Laver, James and Amy de lay Haye. *Costume and Fashion: A Concise History*, Thames and Hudson, 2002.

Newman, Alex and Zakee Shariff. *Fashion A to Z*, Laurence King, 2009.

Rothstein, Natalie, ed. *400 Years of Fashion*, V&A Publishing, 1999.

Sims, Josh. *100 Ideas that Changed Street Style*, Laurence King, 2014.

Worsley, Harriet. *100 Ideas that Changed Fashion*, Laurence King, 2011.

Wilcox, Claire, ed. *Fashion in Detail 1700–2000*, V&A Publishing, 2013.

INDEX

Pages in **bold** refer to illustrations

À bout de souffle (film, Godard, 1960) 105
A-line dresses 66–9
Adams, Maud **54**
Agent Provocateur 134
Alaïa, Azzedine 20, 90
Allen, Barbara **164**
Álvarez, Lilí de 82
And God Created Woman (film, Vadim, 1956) 159
Andress, Ursula 142, **171**
Andrews, Julie 93
Annabella **13**
Anne, Princess **165**
Annie Hall (film, Allen, 1977) 94
Aquascutum 15
Armani, Giorgio 20, **101**
The Artist (film, Hazanavicius, 2011) 188
Ashley, Laura 56, 111 *see also*
    Laura Ashley
Avansino, Calgary (*Vogue*) 161
Avedon, Richard 80, 85
The Avengers (TV show) 27, 147

Baby Doll (film, Kazan, 1956) 46
Bacall, Lauren 31, 147, 198
'Baguette' bags (Fendi) 197
Baker, Josephine 43, 93
Bakst, Léon 64
Balenciaga 165
Ball, Lucille 100
ballet pumps 80, 98, 105, 158–61, 176
Ballets Russes 64
Balmain, Pierre 31, **32**, **37**
Balmain label 76, 106, 174
'Bamboo' bags (Gucci) **195**, 197
Bananarama 80
'Bar' suit (Dior) 71
Bardot, Brigitte 13, 27, **74**, 98, **104**, 105, 124, 143, 159, **160**, 198
Barrie, Jeanne **37**
Barry, Margaret **31**
Bartle Bogle Hegarty 85
Bates, John 27, 116, 147
Bathing Beauty (film, Sidney, 1944) 140
'Bayswater' bags (Mulberry) 197
Bazaar, Kings Road, London 27
Beach Party (film, Asher, 1963) 143
Beachcraft Sandal Company 156
'Beat' collection (Saint Laurent, 1960s) 20
Beaton, Cecil **31**
Beckham, Victoria 15
Beene, Geoffrey **146**
'Beene Bag' collection (Beene, 1975) **146**
Belle de Jour (film, Buñuel, 1967) 44
Bennett, Joan 43
berets **184**, 198–9
Bergdorf Goodman department store 34
Bergman, Ingrid 79, 195
Berlei 112
Bernardini, Micheline 142

Beyoncé 90
Biba 56, 156
biker jackets 19, **21**
bikinis 140, 142–3
Birkin, Jane **92**, **94**, **179**, 197
'Birkin' bag (Hermès) 197
Bissett, Enid 128
Bladerunner (film, Scott, 1982) 33
Blahnik, Manolo **152**, 153, 154
Blanes **46**
Blass, Bill 59, 94
Bloomer, Amelia Jenks 96
blouses 31, 67, 76, 98, 108–11
Bodin 66
'Body Jewellery' collection (Rabanne) 27
Bodymap 80
Bogart, Humphrey 13, 176
bohemian fashion 22, 64, 93, 198
Bonnie and Clyde (film, Penn, 1967) **184**, 198
boots 56, 68, 89–90, 116, 156, 163, 165, 170 *see also* cowboy boots; riding boots
Bottega Veneta 82, 197
Bourdin, Guy **154**
Bow, Clara 54, 195
Bowie, David and Angie 156
The Boy Friend (film, Russell, 1971) 188
Brando, Marlon 19, 75
bras 112, 126–9, **135**
Breakfast at Tiffany's (film, Edwards,1961) **12**, 13, **42**, 44, 49–50, **177**
breton tops 78, 104–7
Bridges, Mark 188
Brooks, Louise 188
Bruce, Liza **133**
Bruni-Sarkozy, Carla 176
Bryant, Louise **174**
Budge, Donald **170**
Buell, Bebe **119**
Bugatti, Ettore 195
Bullocks Wilshire department store 34
Burberry 13, 15
bustiers 116, 134

Cadolle, Herminie 127–8
Callahan, Henry (Lord & Taylor) 131
Calvin Klein label 85
Campbell, Naomi 156
capes 22–3
Capezio 159
Capri pants 80, 98–9
Cardin, Pierre 64, 68, 147, 163
Cassandre 187
Castelnuovo, Nino **13**
Cat on a Hot Tin Roof (film, Brooks, 1958) **130**, 132
Céline 79, 100
Cerruti **92**
Chanel, Gabrielle 'Coco' 38, 43, 59, **78**, 100, 105, 167, **190**, 191, 198
Chanel label 20, **39**, 111, 161, 192, **195**, 197

The Changeling (film, Eastwood, 2008) 188
Charles Jourdan **154**
Charlot, Juli Lynne 34
Cher **121**
'Chérie' dress (Dior) 62
Chloé 197
Christy, C.O. 180
Chung, Alexa **105**
Cifonelli 93
circle skirts 34–5
Claret **68**
Clarks **167**
Clerc, Jean-Louis 187
cloches 188–9, 198
Cole of California 140
'Colombe' dress (Miyake) 71
Connolly, Sybil 71
'Constance' bags (Gucci) 197
Converse 170
Cooper, Charles **68**
Cooper, Gary **110**
Cooper, Jilly 16
Coppola, Sofia **108**
'Corolle' line (Dior, 1947) 67
Corré, Joe (Agent Provocateur) 134
corsets **6**, 31, 53, 109, 127–8, 134–5
costume jewellery 190–3
Courrèges, André 27, **29**, **67**, 68, 94, 147, 165
cowboy boots 163, 172–5
Crawford, Cindy **28**
Crawford, Joan 37, 178
crop tops 114–17
culottes 82–3
Curtis, Jamie Lee **148**
Cyrus, Miley **114**

'Dada' collection (Gaultier, 1983) 134
Danels, Anna-Lee 131
Danskin 148
Davis, Bette 13
Day, Doris 98
Dayton, Warren 118
De Carlo, Yvonne 174
De la Renta, Oscar 56, 64
De Lennart, Sonja 98
De Losques **109**
De Medici, Catherine 154
DeHavilland, Terry 156
'Delphos' dress (Fortuny) 70
Demarchelier, Patrick **97**, **152**
DeMille, Cecil B. 168
Deneuve, Catherine **13**, 15, **43**, 44
Desperately Seeking Susan (film, Seidelman, 1985) 127
Dessès, Jean 71
Diaghialev, Serge 64
The Dick Van Dyke Show (TV show) 98
Dietrich, Marlene 54, 93, **94**, 112, 182, 188, **189**, 195, 198
Dillon, Matt 19
DiMaggio, Joe 53

Dior, Christian **22**, 28, **30**, 31, 34, 37, 62, 67, 71, 165
Dior label **26**, 67, **88**, 124, 153
'divided skirts' 82
Dolce & Gabbana 22, **33**, 90, 134, 147
Donovan, Terence **107**
Dr. No (film, Young, 1962) 142
Dress for Success (book, Molloy) 38
The Dukes of Hazzard (TV show) 90
Dumas, Jean-Louis (Hermès) 197
Dumas, Robert (Hermès) 195
Dunaway, Faye **184**, 198
Duncan, Isadora 185

Earhart, Amelia 93
Eastwood, Clint 22
Eden, Barbara 115
Eisenhower, Julie Nixon 59
Ekberg, Anita **98**
Elizabeth II, Queen 112, 185
Elizabeth of Bavaria, Empress of Austria **16**
Emilioform 147
empire-line dresses 46–7, 56

Faithful, Marianne **76**
Fame (TV show) 149
Farrow, Mia **49**, 50
Fath, Jacques 31, 67
Fendi 197
Ferragamo, Salvatore 100, 156, **167**, 168, 176, 178, 180
'Fête' collection (Miyake, 2004) 71
Flashdance (film, Lyne, 1983) 80, 149
Flory, Régine **70**
Flower Materials 192
flying jackets 19–20, **105**
Foale & Tuffin 112
Fogarty, Anne 62
Fonda, Bridget 19
Ford, Lita 75
The Forsyte Saga (TV show) 56
Fortuny, Mariano 70
Foster, Jodie 90
Frowick, Roy Halston *see* Halston
The Fugitive Kind (film, Lumet, 1960) 75
Funicello, Annette 143
Funny Face (film, Donen, 1957) 80, 98, **99**, 105, 112, 159, 176

Gainsbourg, Charlotte 15
Gainsbourg, Serge **92**
Galitzine, Irene 78, 147
Galliano, John **88**, 132
Garbo, Greta 13, 54, 178, 198
Gardner, Ava 13, 98, **136**
Garland, Judy **24**, 156, 180
Gaultier, Jean-Paul 127, **128**, 134, 149
Gernreich, Rudi 63, 140
Gibb, Bill 22, 56
'Gibson Girl' (Charles Gibson) 109
Gilda (film, Vidor, 1946) 44

Gish, Lillian 70
Givenchy, Hubert de 44, 49–50, 98
Givenchy label 147
Glaser, Milton 118
Gomes, Maria Teresinha (Tito) 93
Gore, Angela 56
Grable, Betty 89, 140, **143**
Grant, Allen (Glen Raven Knitting Mills) 124
Grant, Cary 106
Grease (film, Kleiser, 1978) 100
Greenberg, Adrian Adolf 37
Gregory **111**
grunge fashion 19, 46, 132, 170
Gucci 106, **195**, 197
Gynt, Greta **167**

H-line skirts (Dior) 31, 67
Hall, Jerry **164**
Hall, Radclyffe 82
Halston 54, 63, 64, 100
halter-neck dresses 52–5
Hammer, MC 96
Hamnett, Katharine 90, 118
Hansen, Maya **80**
Hardy, Françoise **21**, 94
harem pants 78, 96–7
Harlow, Jean 54, 198
'Harris Tweed' collection (Westwood, 1987) 16
Harry, Debbie (Blondie) **77**, **125**
Haskell, Miriam 192, **193**
Hayworth, Rita 44, 140
Head, Edith 98, 106, 176, 195
Heavenly Bodies (film, Jackson, 1984) 149
Heim, Jacques 142
Hennink, Marpessa **33**, **127**
Hepburn, Audrey **9**, 38, **102**, 105, **110**, 187, 192, **196**, 197
    Breakfast at Tiffany's **12**, 13, **42**, 44, 49–50, **177**
    Funny Face 80, 98, **99**, 105, 112, 159, 176
    Roman Holiday 98, 159, 176
    Sabrina 98, **158**, 159, 176
Hepburn, Katharine 13, 54, 78, 93, 100, 111, 147, **170**
Hermès 22, 185, 187, **194**, 195, 197
Hermès, Emile-Maurice 195
Herzigova, Eva 128
Hilfiger, Tommy 100
hippie fashion 22, 38, 64, 86, 116, 118, 120, 168
hobble skirts 31, 33
Holah, David (Bodymap) 80
Hollywood and fashion 13, 15, 37, 54, 98, 140, 159, 168, 173–4, 178, 192
hot pants 28, 76, 88–91
'Hot Pants' (song, Brown, 1971) 89
Hughes, Howard 127
Hulanicki, Barbara (Biba) 56, 156
Hurley, Elizabeth 44

Hyer Boot Company 174
Hynde, Chrissie (The Pretenders) **18**, 75, **76**, **118**

I Dream of Jeannie (TV show) 115
I Love Lucy (TV show) 100
'Intrecciato' bags (Bottega Veneta) 197
The Iron Petticoat (film, Thomas, 1956) 13
Irvin jackets 19
'it bags' 194–7
'Itsy Bitsy Teenie Weenie Yellow Polka Dot Bikini' (song, Hyland, 1960) 143

Jacob, Mary Phelps 128
Jacobs, Marc 79, 82, 174
Jagger, Bianca **53**, 54, 79, **94**, 156, **157**
James, Henry 43
Jane Fonda's Workout (book and video, 1982) 80, 149
Jantzen, Carl 143
jeans 76, 84–7, 105, 159, 170
Jett, Joan 75
Jolie, Angelina **188**
Jordan 19
Josephine, Empress of France 46, 167, 185
jumpsuits 144–7

kaftans 64–5, 96
Kahlo, Frida 93
Kamali, Norma 80, 147
Kangol 198
Karan, Donna 149
Keaton, Diane 94
Kellerman, Annette 143
Kelly, Grace 31, 38, 64, 112, 187, **192**, **194**, 195
Kelly, Patrick 188
Kelly bags (Hermès) **194**, 195, 197
Kempner, Nan 94
Kennedy, Jacqueline (later Onassis) 13, 38, 44, **49**, 50, 105, 192, 197
Keyes, Alicia **175**
kitten heels 98, 176–7
Kleid, Murray (S&M Fringing) 120
Klein, Calvin 50, 76, 86, 94 *see also* Calvin Klein
Koscina, Sylvia **149**
Krebs, Germains (Madame Alix Grès) 71

Lady Gaga **155**
Laforêt, Marie **65**
Lake, Veronica 78, 147
Lamour, Dorothy 140
Lane, Kenneth Jay **191**, 192
Lang, Helmut **50**
Lanvin-Costello **66**
The Last Days of Disco (film, Stillman, 1998) 120
Lauper, Cindi 80
Laura Ashley label 56, **57**, **62**
Lauren, Ralph 16, 56, 63, 94, 96
'Le Smoking' suit (Saint Laurent) 94

leather jackets 18–21
leather trousers 74–7
Leave It to Beaver (TV show) 62
leggings 76, 80–1, 116
Leigh, Janet **187**
Leigh, Vivien **45**, 192
Lennox, Annie (Eurythmics) 93
Leone, Sergio 22
Léotard, Jules 148
leotards 80, 148–9
Leser, Tina 115
Lesher, Henry 128
Levi jeans 54, 85–6, 170
Liberty of London 185, 188
Lick, Don 118
'Lilly' dress 49
'the little black dress' 13, 42–5, 59, 62
Little House on the Prairie (TV show) 56
Lively, Blake **47**
Locklear, Heather **144**
logos 116, 118, **119**, 187
Lollobrigida, Gina **126**
Lombard, Carole 78
Lopez, Jennifer **64**, **88**
Lord & Taylor 131
Loren, Sophia **91**, 98, 112
Louboutin, Christian 154, 163, **176**, **178**
Louis Vuitton label **196**, 197
'lounge pants' 78, 100
Love, Courtney (Hole) 46, 132, **132**
Lutyens, Eva **31**

Mad Men (TV show) 112
Madonna 80, 93, 116, **117**, 127, **128**, 134, 147, **148**, 149
Maidenform 112, 128
Maier, Tomas 197
Maison IRFE **120**
Mansfield, Jayne 112, **122**, 143
Marant, Isabel 76, 180
Margill **134**
Marlohe, Bérénice **59**
Mary Tudor, Queen 154
McCardell, Claire 59, 71, 86, 115, 159
McCartney, Stella 82, 100, 147
McLaren, Malcolm 19
McQueen, Alexander 22, 86
Mellinger, Frederick (Frederick's of Hollywood) 128
menswear, adopting 13, 16, 19–20, 37, 63, 75, 85, 93–4, 100, 165, 198
Mercury, Freddie (Queen) 149
Michael, Arthur C. **139**
Michahelles, Ernesto (Thayaht) 145
Middleton, Kate (Duchess of Cambridge) 15, **38**
military influences on fashion 15, 16, 19–20, 63, 106, 118, 145, 163, 198
Miller, Ann **140**, 178
Miller, Lee 93
minidresses *see* miniskirts
The Miniskirt Rebellion (TV show, ABC, 1967) 28
miniskirts 26–9, 33, 46, 50, 56, 63, 68, 89, 116, 124

Minnelli, Liza 54
Minogue, Kylie 90, 134
Miranda, Carmen **150**, 156, **157**, 178
The Misfits (film, Huston, 1961) **84**, 86
Missoni 22
Mitchum, Robert 13
Miyake, Issey **70**, 71, 96
Molloy, John 38
Molyneux, Edward 43, 78, **96**, 100
Monaghan, Josephine 93
Mondrian dress (Saint Laurent) 50, **51**
Monroe, Marilyn **31**, **72**, **84**, 86, 89, 98, 105, 112, **138**, 143, 153, 174, 180
    The Seven Year Itch 53, 70, **71**
Montana, Claude **19**, 76
Montano, Mark 22
'Moon Girl' collection (Courrèges, 1964) 68
Moore, Mary Tyler 98
Moreau, Jeanne 105
Mori, Hanae **68**
Morrison, Jim (The Doors) 75
Moss, Kate 15, 132, **133**, 174
Mouse, Stanley 118
Mugler, Thierry 20, 76, 134, 147
Mulberry 197
Mulder, Karen 93, **107**, **135**
music and fashion 75–6, 93, 96, 116, 118, 147, 149, 159, 170, 174
Myra Breckinridge (film, Same, 1970) **172**

Nadler, Michael **34**
Napoleon I (Napoleon Bonaparte) 46, 154, 185
Neiman Marcus department store 34, **86**
New Look (Dior) 31, 34, 62, 67, 165
Newton-John, Olivia 80, 149
Nijinsky, Vaslav 148
Nike 170, 180
No More Ladies (film, Griffith, 1935) 37
Novak, Kim 38, 105

Obama, Michelle **161**, 176
O'Connor, Erin **50**
Of Human Bondage (film, Cromwell, 1934) 13
Onassis, Jacqueline Kennedy *see* Kennedy, Jacqueline
One Million Years B.C. (film, Chaffey, 1966) 143
Ono, Yoko **90**
The Outlaw (film, Hughes, 1943) 127

'Paddington' bags (Chloé) 197
pajama pants 100–1
palazzo pants 78–9, 100, 147
Parker, Jean **35**
Parker, Sarah-Jessica **120**
Parker, Suzy **193**
Parton, Dolly 174, **175**
Pasche, John 118
Patou, Jean 115
Pearce, Jacqueline **47**
peep-toes 178–9
pencil skirts 30–3, 37
Peppard, George **12**, 13

Rebel (film, Bridges, 1985) **118**
Perfecto biker jackets 19
Persil advertisement **112**
Perugia, André 153
Petty, George 89, 168
Physical Culture magazine **149**
Pignatelli, Principessa Luciana **192**
platforms 90, 156–7, 168, 176, 178, **179**, 180
pleated dresses 70–1
pleated skirts 34, 56, 62, 67, 70
'Pleats Please' line (Miyake, 1993) 71
plimsolls 170–1
Poiret, Paul 22, 33, 64, 78, 96, 100, 134, 165
Poirier, Louise 128
Polo (book, Cooper) 16
ponchos 22
'poodle skirts' 34
'popover' dress (McCardell) 59, 86
Portland Knitting Company 139
power dressing 28, 33, 38, 56, 94
Prada 120, 147, 197
prairie dresses 56–7
Prendergast, Tessa 142
The Price is Right (TV show) 120
Pringle of Scotland 112
Pucci, Emilio 22, 64, 79, **100**, 147
Pulitzer, Lilly **48**, 49
punk fashion 19–20, 28, 134, 170
pyjamas and pyjama suits 78, 100, 116

Quant, Mary 27–8, 33, 50, 68, 89, 112, 124, 198, **199**
Quatro, Suzi 75, 147
Queen Kelly (film, von Stroheim, 1929) 13

Rabanne, Paco 27
Rahl, Mady 98
Rampling, Charlotte 15
rationing and fashion 31, 34, 37–8, 44, 62–3, 128, 143, 159, 180
Une Ravissante Idiote (film, Molinaro, 1964) 13
Rear Window (film, Hitchcock, 1954) 38
Réard, Louis 142
Reboux, Caroline 188, 198
Repetto 159, **160**, 161
'Resort' collection (Armani, 2008) **101**
Reynolds, Debbie 53, **81**
Rice, Ernest 124
Riders (book, Cooper) 16
riding boots 162–5
riding jackets 16–7
Rigg, Diana 27, 147
Rihanna **20**
'Rive Gauche' dress (Saint Laurent) **43**
Rockwell, Norman **147**
Rodchenko, Aleksandr 145
Rogers, Ginger **15**, 54
Rolfe, Colin 27
Rolled Stockings (film, Rosson, 1927) **124**
Roman Holiday (film, Wyler, 1953) 98, 159, 176
Rose, Helen 132

Rosenthal, Ida and William 128
'Rosie the Riveter' (Rockwell) 147
Ross, Diana **111**
Roth, David Lee (Van Halen) 149
Russell, Jane **52**, 98, 112, 127, 192

Sabrina (film, Wilder, 1954) 98, **158**, 159, 176
Saint James 106
Saint Laurent, Yves 20, 28, **40**, **43**, 50, **51**, 64, 67, 94, 96, 100, 147 *see also* Yves Saint Laurent
sandals 166–9
scarves 185, 187
Scheherazade (ballet) 64
Schiaparelli, Elsa **38**, 71, 82, **83**, 93, 145, 147, 156, 187
Schott Bros. 19
Scianna, Ferdinando **127**
Seberg, Jean 105
Sedgwick, Edie 105
The Seven Year Itch (film, Wilder, 1955) 53, 70, **71**
sewing patterns 34, **44**, 56, 63, 67, 89, 111
Sex, London 19
sex and fashion 16, 53–4, 75, 85, 89–90, 124, 134, 153, 176, 178
Sex and the City (TV show) 120
Shields, Brooke **85**
shift dresses 48–51
shirt dresses (shirtwaisters) 62–3, 86
Shrimpton, Jean 27
'Signature' collection (Halston, 2002) **100**
silk scarves 184–7
Simon, Carly **166**
Simpson, Jessica 174
Simpson, Wallis (Duchess of Windsor) 43, 188
Singles (film, Crowe, 1992) 19
Siouxsie Sioux 19
skirt suits 36–9
Skyfall (film, Mendes, 2012) **59**
sling backs 178–9
slips 130–3
'Sloane Rangers' 111
S&M Fringing, New York 120
Some Like It Hot (film, Wilder, 1959) 31
Spears, Britney 116, 120, 174
Spencer, Diana (Princess Diana) **56**
sport and fashion 82, 93, 96, 109, 139–40, 148–9, **163**, 170, 198 *see also* workout gear
Sportscraft **31**
Stanwyck, Barbara **53**
Stefani, Gwen 116
Stepanova, Vavara 145
Stewart, Stevie (Bodymap) 80
stilettos 76, 152–5, 176
stockings 27, 28, 63, 124, 134, 165, 167–8, 178
street style 27, 80, **98**, 149, **181**
suits *see* skirt suits; trouser suits
Swanson, Gloria 13
'sweater girls' 112, 128
Swift, Taylor **63**

swimming costumes 53, 115, 120, 138–43, **185** *see also* bikinis
'Swinging London' 27–8, 116, 198

T-shirts 116, **117**, 118–9, 132, 170
Tahari, Elie 120
Tallien, Madame 167
'Tanger' cape (Poiret) 22
Taxi Driver (film, Scorsese, 1976) 90
Taylor, Charles ('Chuck') 170
Taylor, Elizabeth 31, **55**, 64, 98, **130**, 132, 187, 192
teenage fashion 34, 86, 112, 159, 170, **173**, 176
Thatcher, Margaret 111, 118
They Won't Forget (film, LeRoy, 1937) 112, 128
Thorgerson, Storm 118
Tierney, Gene **185**
tights 27, 28, 80, 124–5
Tiziani Boutique **192**
To Catch a Thief (film, Hitchcock, 1955) 106, **192**, 195
'Trapeze' collection (Saint Laurent, 1958) 67
Travilla, William 53, 70
trench coats 12–5
Triumph 112
'Tropical Togs' line (Levi's, 1938) 54
trouser suits 92–5
tube tops 116, 120–1, **192**
Tucck, Maric 128
Turner, Lana 112, 128, **145**
Turner, Tina 75
Twiggy **8**, **27**, 46, 50, **186**, **198**
twinsets 112–3

The Umbrellas of Cherbourg (film, Demy, 1964) **13**
underwear as outerwear 100, 127, 131, 134
Ungaro, Emanuel 68
Upstairs Downstairs (TV show) 56

Valentino 64, 111, 147
Van Runkle, Theodora 198
Vanderbilt, Wendy **48**
Vanity Fair 16
Vargas, Alberto 89, 168, **169**
Verninac, Madame Raymond de **46**
Versace, Donatella **28**
Versace, Gianni 20, 44, **135**
Versace label 76, 120
Vertigo (film, Hitchcock, 1958) 38
Vicious, Sid (Sex Pistols) 19
Victor/Victoria (film, Edwards, 1982) 93
Vionnet, Madeleine 53, 115, 131, 167
Vivier, Roger **152**, 153, 156, 165
Von Fürstenberg, Diane **58**, 59–60, **60**, **61**, 100
Vreeland, Diana (*Vogue*) 59, 64, 78, 120
Vuitton, Louis 100 *see also* Louis Vuitton label

Wanted **180**
Warner 128

Weatherbee trench coats **14**
wedges 180–1
Weisz, Otto 112
Welch, Raquel 143, **172**
The Well of Loneliness (Hall, 1928) 82
Wellington boots 163, 165
Westwood, Vivienne 16, **17**, 19, 134, 156
Whitney, Alice and Nancy **16**
Wife Dressing (book, Fogarty) 62
The Wild One (film, Benedek, 953) 19
Williams, Esther 89, **115**, 140, 143
The Wings of the Dove (book, James) 43
Wintour, Anna (*Vogue*) 132
Wolsey twinset **113**
A Woman of Affairs (film, Brown, 1928) 13
The Woman's Dress for Success Book (Molloy) 38
Wonderbra 128
Wood, Natalie 105
Woodward, Joanne 13
Working Girl (film, Nichols, 1988) 38
workout gear and fashion 80, 116, 148–9
Wrangler 86
wrap dresses 58–61

Y-line skirts (Dior) 67
Yamamoto, Yohji 71, 147
Yves Saint Laurent label 47, **93**, 165

PICTURE CREDITS

4 Alan Band/Keystone/Getty Images; 6 Horst P. Horst/The Condé Nast Publications; 7 Frances McLaughlin-Gill/The Condé Nast Publications; 8 Roger-Viollet/Rex Features; 9 Getty Images; 10 John Rawlings/ The Condé Nast Publications; 12 Franco Rubartelli/ The Condé Nast Publications; 13 (left) Kobal; 13 (right) Everett Collection/Rex Features; 14 ; 15 (left) Max Mumby/ Indigo/Getty Images; 15 (right) John Kobal Foundation/Getty Images; 16 (Top) Hulton Archive/Getty Images; 16 (bottom) Bert Morgan/Getty Images; 17 David Cheskin/PA Archive/Press Association Images; 18 Fin Costello/ Redferns/Getty Images; 19 (left) Moviestore Collection/Rex Features; 19 (right) Daniel SIMON/Gamma-Rapho via Getty Images; 20 (left) Mr Hartnett/PYMCA/Rex Features; 20 (right) Kevin Winter/Getty Images; 21 Reg Lancaster/Express/Getty Images; 22 (top) Frank Barratt/Keystone/Getty Images; 22 (bottom) Bruno Barbey/ Magnum Photos; 23 Chaloner Woods/ Getty Images; 24 Silver Screen Collection/Hulton Archive/Getty Images; 26 Larry Ellis/Express/Getty Images; 27 (left) Bettmann/CORBIS; 27 (right) Hulton Archive/Getty Images; 28 (left) Terry O'Neill/Getty Images; 28 (right) Giovanni Giannoni/ The Condé Nast Publications; 29 Jack Garofalo/Paris Match via Getty Images; 30 KAMMERMAN/Gamma-Rapho via Getty Images; 31 (left) Philippe Halsman/Magnum Photo; 31 (right) Cecil Beaton/ The Condé Nast Publications; 32 AP/Press Association Images; 33 Ferdinando Scianna/ Magnum Photos; 34 (top) TopFoto; 34 (bottom) Popperfoto/Getty Images; 35 Popperfoto/Getty Images; 36 John Rawlings/ The Condé Nast Publications; 37 (left) Henry Clarke/ The Condé Nast Publications; 37 (right) Toni Frissell/ The Condé Nast Publications; 38 (top) Raymond de Lavererie/ The Condé Nast Publications; 38 (bottom) David Cheskin/PA Archive/Press Association Images; 39 PIERRE GUILLAUD/AFP/ Getty Images; 40 Sabine WEISS/ Gamma-Rapho via Getty Images; 42 Rex Features; 43 Reg Lancaster/Getty Images; 44 (left) Richard Young/Rex features; 44 (right) Frances McLaughlin-Gill/ The Condé Nast Publications; 45 Silver Screen Collection/Getty Images; 46 (top) Barratts/S&G Barratts/ EMPICS Archive; 46 (bottom) Getty Images; 47 (left) Erik C. Pendzich/Rex Features; 47 (right) Popperfoto/Getty Images; 48 Slim Aarons/Hulton Archive/Getty Images; 49 (left) Paul Schutzer/Time & Life Pictures/Getty Images; 49 (right) Max B. Miller/Fotos International/Getty Images; 50 The Condé Nast Publications; 51 Sipa Press/ Rex Features; 52 Silver Screen Collection/Getty Images; 53 (left) Ron Galella/WireImage/Getty Images; 53 (right) John Kobal Foundation/Getty Images; 54 (left) Susan Wood/Getty Images; 54 The Condé Nast Publications; 55 Silver Screen Collection/Getty Images; 56 (top) Richard Young/Rex Features; 56 (bottom) Moviestore Collection/Rex Features; 57 By kind permission of Laura Ashley Ltd; 58 Rex Features; 59 Moviestore Collection/Rex Features; 60 (left) Petre Buzoianu/Corbis; 60 (right) AFP/Getty Images; 61 Peter Foley/ Corbis; 62 (top) By kind permission of Laura Ashley Ltd; 62 (bottom) Chaloner Woods/Getty Images; 63 Rex Features; 64 AKM-GSI/ /Splash News/ Corbis; 65 Raymond Depardon/ Magnum Photos; 66 Keystone-France/ Gamma-Keystone via Getty Images; 67 Bill Ray/Time Life Pictures/Getty Images; 68 Bern Stern/The Condé Nast Publications; 69 David McCabe/The Condé Nast Publications; 70 (left) Reuters/Corbis; 70 (right) Roger-Viollet / Topfoto; 71 Everett Collection/c.20thC.Fox/Rex Features; 72 Eve Arnold/Magnum Photos; 74 Ghislain DUSSART/Gamma-Rapho via Getty Images; 75 Brian McCreeth/Rex Features; 76 (left) Tom Pilston/The Independent/Rex Features; 76 (right) Keystone/Getty Images; 77 Michael Brennan/Getty Images; 78 Time Life Pictures/Getty Images; 79 Henry Clarke/The Condé Nast Publications; 80 Juan Naharro Gimenez/WireImage/ Getty Images; 81 Silver Screen Collection/Getty Images; 82 Topical Press Agency/Getty Images; 83 (top) Henry Clarke/The Condé Nast Publications; 83 (bottom) Hulton-Deutsch Collection/CORBIS; 84 Eve Arnold/Magnum Photos; 85 Calvin Klein advertisement courtesy of Calvin Klein, photograph © The Richard Avedon Foundation; 86 (left) Bettmann/ CORBIS; 86 (right) Monica Mcklinski/ Getty Images; 87 John Aquino/The Condé Nast Publications; 88 Guy Marineau/The Condé Nast Publications; 89 (left) Startraks Photo/Rex Features; 89 (right) Alan Band/Keystone/Getty Images; 90 (left) Steve Schapiro/Corbis; 90 (right) Simins Peter/The Condé Nast Publications; 91 David Seymour/ Magnum Photos; 92 Nicolas Tikhomiroff/Magnum Photos; 93 PIERRE VERDY/AFP/Getty Images; 94 (left) Time Life Pictures/Getty Images; 94 (right) Bob Thomas/ Popperfoto/Getty Images; 95 Express Newspapers/Getty Images; 96 Mary Evans Picture Library; 97 Patrick Demarchelier/ The Condé Nast Publications; 98 (top) Gene Lester/Getty Images; 98 (bottom) Catherine Farrell/ WireImage/Getty Images; 99 Ronald Grant Archive; 100 (top) Lawrence Lucier/Getty Images; 100 (bottom) David Lees//Time Life Pictures/Getty Images; 101 Dave Yoder/Conde Nast; 102 Everett Collection/Rex Features; 104 Willy Rizzo/Paris Match via Getty Images; 105 (left) RDA/Hulton Archive/ Getty Images; 105 (right) Splash News/ Corbis; 106 Nina Leen/Time & Life Pictures/Getty Images; 107 Terence Donovan Archive/Getty Images; 108 Rob Kim/Getty Images; 109 (left) Time Life Pictures/Mansell/Time Life Pictures/Getty Images; 109 (right) Archive Photos/Getty Images; 110 Everett Collection/Rex Features; 111 (top) Karlin Lynn/The Condé Nast Publications; 111 (bottom) Gianni Penati/The Condé Nast Publications; 112 (top) Picture Post/Hulton Archive/ Getty Images; 112 (bottom) Tim Graham/Getty Images; 113 Chaloner Woods/Getty Images; 114 Startraks Photo/Rex Features; 115 (left) Everett Collection/Rex Features; 115 (right) Silver Screen Collection/Getty Images; 116 Reuters/CORBIS; 117 Jim Steinfeldt/Michael Ochs Archives/Getty Images; 118 (top) Michael Putland/ Getty Images; 118 (bottom) Neil Munns/PA Archive/Press Association Images; 119 Michael Ochs Archives/ Getty Images; 120 (top) Victor Boyko/ Getty images for IRFE Paris; 120 (bottom) Everett/c.HBO/Rex Features; 121 CBS Photo Archive/Getty Images; 122 Weegee(Arthur Fellig)/International Center of Photography/Getty Images; 124 Buyenlarge/Getty Images; 125 Maureen Donaldson/Getty Images; 126 Pierluigi Praturlon/Rex Features; 127 (left) United Artists/Archive Photos/ Getty Images; 127 (right) Ferdinando Scianna/Magnum Photos; 128 Eugene Adebari/Rex Features; 129 PA/ Tophams/Topham Picturepoint/Press Association Images; 130 Everett

Collection/Rex Features; **131** Eduardo Garcia Benito/ The Condé Nast Publications; **132** Fred Prouser/Reuters/Corbis; **133** RICHARD YOUNG/Rex Features; **134** (**top**) Stebbing/Henry Guttmann/Getty Images; **134** (**bottom**) GILL ALLEN/AP/Press Association Images; **135** Guy Marineau/The Condé Nast Publications; **136** John Kobal Foundation/Getty Images; **138** Eve Arnold/Magnum Photos; **139** SSPL/Getty Images; **140**(**top**) Peter Kramer/Getty Images; **140** (**bottom**) Everett Collection/Rex Features; **141** Bourgeron Collection/RDA/Hulton Archive/Getty Images; **142** Moviestore Collection/Rex Features; **143** (**left**) Everett Collection/Rex Features; **143** (**right**) Sipa Press/Rex Features; **144** Harry Langdon/Getty Images; **145** Hulton Archive/Getty Images; **146** AP/AP/Press Association Images; **147** "Rosie the Riveter" illustration provided by SEPS. All Rights Reserved" & Printed by permission of the Norman Rockwell Family Agency. Copyright © the Norman Rockwell Family Entities; **148** (**left**) Rex Features **148**(**right**) Everett Collection/Rex Features; **149** (**left**) Transcendental Graphics/Getty Images; **149** (**right**) Marisa Rastellini/Mondadori Portfolio via Getty Images; **150** Everett Collection/Rex Features; **152** Patrick Demarchalier/The Condé Nast Publications; **153** Manolo Blahnik; **154** Guy Bourdin/Art & Commerce; **155** Jamie McCarthy/Getty Images; **156** **Courtesy Museo Salvatore Ferragamo, Florence; 157** (**top**) Everett Collection/Rex Features; **157** (**bottom**) Christopher Simon Sykes/Hulton Archive/Getty Images; **158** SNAP/Rex Features; **159** Everett Collection/Rex Features; **160** (**top**) TopFoto / UPP; **160** (**bottom**) JACKY NAEGELEN/Reuters/Corbis; **161** Rex Features; **162** Land Lost Content / HIP / TopFoto; **163** Keystone/Getty Images; **164** MEDIA PRESS/REX; **165** (**left**) Keystone-France/Gamma-Keystone via Getty Images; **165** (**right**) Bettmann/CORBIS; **166** Jack Robinson/Hulton Archive/Getty Images; **167** (**left**) SSPL/Getty Images; **167**(**right**) Courtesy Museo Salvatore Ferragamo, Florence; **168** Herbert Gehr/Life Magazine/Time & Life Pictures/Getty Images; **169** (**both**) Snap/Rex Features; **169**(**top**) Victoria and Albert Museum, London; **170** Mondadori Portfolio via Getty Images; **171** Jean-Claude Deutsch/Paris Match via Getty Images; **172** Terry O'Neill/Getty Images; **173** (**left**) Peter Stackpole/Life Magazine/Time & Life Pictures/Getty Images; **173** (**right**) Danny Lehman/Corbis; **174** Evening Standard/Getty Images; **175** (**left**) Henry Lamb/BEI/Rex Features; **175** (**right**) Kathryn Osler/The Denver Post via Getty Images; **176** Mousse - Orban Thierry/ABACA/Press Association Images; **177** Snap/Rex Features; **178** Fairchild Photo Service/Condé Nast/Corbis; **179** Rex Features; **180** (**top**) John Aquino/The Condé Nast Publications; **180** (**bottom**) Courtesy Museo Salvatore Ferragamo, Florence; **181** Timur Emek/Getty Images; **182** Snap/Rex Features; **184** Everett Collection/Rex Features; **185** (**left**) Silver Screen Collection/Getty Images; **185** (**right**) Kasia Wandycz/Paris Match via Getty Images; **186** Justin de Villeneuve/Hulton Archive/Getty Images; **187** Hulton Archive/Getty Images; **188** Everett Collection/Universal/Rex Features; **189** Corbis; **190** Lipnitzki/Roger Viollet/Getty Images; **191** J.Gwendolynne Berry/ZUMA Press/Corbis; **192** (**top**) Henry Clarke/The Condé Nast Publications; **192** (**bottom**) Everett Collection/Rex Features; **193** Conde Nast/Corbis; **194** Howard Sochurek/Time & Life Pictures/Getty Images; **195** (**top**) Stephane Cardinale/People Avenue/Corbis; **195** (**bottom**) Elena Braghieri/Getty Images; **196** Everett Collection/Rex Features; **197** Michel Dufour/WireImage/Getty Images; **198** (**top**) Hulton-Deutsch Collection/CORBIS; **198** (**bottom**) Everett Collection/Rex Features; **199** Keystone France/Gamma-Keystone via Getty Images